the
KEY
to the
HIDDEN

—

THE WISDOM OF THE DRUIDS
THE SWASTIKA
THE PACT WITH NATURE
MERLIN THE MAGICIAN
THE LEGEND OF THE GRAIL
THE MYSTERY OF TAROT
THE ARK OF SOLOMON'S TEMPLE
THE MISSION OF THE BOHEMIANS
THE SECRET OF BUDDHA AND JESUS

Discovery Publisher

Original title: La Clef des Choses Cachées
2015, Discovery Publisher

©2018, Discovery Publisher

Author: Maurice Magre
Translator: Nathalie Glowaty
Editor: Adriano Lucca

616 Corporate Way
Valley Cottage, New York, 10989
www.discoverypublisher.com
edition@discoverypublisher.com
facebook.com/discoverypublisher
twitter.com/discoverypb

New York • Paris • Dublin • Tokyo • Hong Kong

TABLE OF CONTENTS

the
KEY
to the
HIDDEN

—

THE WISDOM OF THE DRUIDS
THE SWASTIKA
THE PACT WITH NATURE
MERLIN THE MAGICIAN
THE LEGEND OF THE GRAIL
THE MYSTERY OF TAROT
THE ARK OF SOLOMON'S TEMPLE
THE MISSION OF THE BOHEMIANS
THE SECRET OF BUDDHA AND JESUS

Foreword

I admired this anonymous poet, author of a novel of chivalry on the Holy Grail, and I dreamed of being his of course. It was the night of the Good Friday, he said, seven hundred and seventeen years after the Passion of Jesus Christ and he was sitting alone in his room, at the end of one of the lost villages of Brittany and its beautiful stones.

Suddenly, he heard his name being called and saw in front of him a pale young man with bright eyes, and of a surprising beauty. He fell down, fainting with emotion. In those distant times, human sensitivity was probably more vivid than today. Then the young man approached and gave him a "precious among all" book on the first page of which the poet read: "Here begins the story of the Holy Grail."

I always dreamed of a pale and very handsome young man holding a book. It is in my mind, in a confused state, a poet enamored by the beauty of mysterious things and who has a greater faith than mine. For faith is an essential element to discover what is worthy of being loved. The anonymous poet who fell fainting on the night of the Good Friday, in the eighth century, had begun to doubt. He doubted, he says, the reality of the dogma of the Holy Trinity. Maybe it is necessary to start having doubts in order to have the visit of the young man.

I, too, doubted. I doubted the real existence of this mysterious Grail, this emerald cup full of a mystical blood about which the anonymous poet had to embroider so many extraordinary adventures, and often boring. And I doubted not only its real existence but also the symbol it concealed.

For the Grail, the cup where, according to the legend, was collected the blood of Jesus, is only the symbol of a superior knowledge. Has this knowledge circulated since the beginning of the world, have wise men transmitted it among themselves and has it been called the Grail when it was the own truth of the wise Jesus? I doubted at first and on the evening of the Good Friday, no young man came to give me an occult book.

But to fell into a swoon, in front of a vision, on a lonely night, is certainly not the best method to know. It is only the sign of a charming but excessive sensitivity. I fallowed step by step, through a narrow path in the forest of books, the track of men who didn't want to talk about themselves, who didn't build monuments, who wore ordinary cloths and did not seek power. Those men who, a few centuries later, must have had the same exterior appearance, have passed what is best in humanity.

Those who consider only historical documents, the reality of their signatures and the shortsighted narrowness of their vision, shook their heads when it was question not of the existence, but of the actual parentage of these beings. Yet, their vestige exists. It is rather a floating luminosity in the shadows than a tangible certainty. To recognize it, it is necessary to develop the faculty of perceiving light glimmers, the barely traced indications.

And after a long search, in pursuit of these torches lost in the past and those who carried them, I realized that there was no more space in me for doubt and that the young man came to visit me without my knowledge.

I was instructed on the Grail, on his legend and his inner truth. I knew that the Druids had know it long before Joseph of Arimathea had put himself in march westward, that the seven Rishis Indous had know it before the Druids, and that there had been on the whole earth, small communities to worship it. I followed with love these communities. I almost touched the linen of which are weaved the robes of pure men. I saw light the sacred fire in the middle of the forest. I heard the ravens fly away when were handed the auspicious words. I sailed toward Avalon, the island of Cypress, with Merlin. I climbed with Parsifal the chaste, the slopes of Montségur, in Ariège.

By dint of living with the thought of these superior men, unknown and deliberately locked in their mission as in a diamond tower, through brushing against their presence, glimpsing the whiteness of their silhouette, I ended up with nostalgia for these superhuman friends. I indulged in waiting for a miraculous visit, I hoped for what life is not giving, the arrival of the superior man whose word fulfills the dream of your intelligence. But I knew that the wait itself is benefactress and to listen in the silence of some doorbell night that never resonates, one gains an unexpected knowledge of oneself.

Christ's blood was poured into a sacred cup long before the birth of Jesus. It has circulated and it will circulate forever through the selflessness of a few man who have received the mission to carry it age to age.

I feel privileged by a sort of grace for having walked behind the silent shadows of these men, tried to name those who have not wanted to wore one, a form to those who have not attached much importance to the physical appearance. But I think the one who will be even more favored is the one who, by a natural outpouring of the soul, without help of any book, without sitting at any round table between forty nine knights of the spirit, will bring out in his heart the secret light of the Grail.

THE WISDOM OF THE DRUIDS

The Cliché of the Druids

There is a great sadness in observing how, sometimes, in history, the greatest of achievements are destroyed by the brute force of cynical incomprehension. And this destruction would be of little concern, for the spirit will remain even after its material form has disappeared. But what is enraging, is to perceive the trace of a dark and hypocritical force which, with a sort of obscure wisdom, works patiently to destroy the truth, to distort it when it appears in its pure form, to make it a caricature of itself.

The methods of this force are numerous: a calumny flying from mouth to mouth which is passed down through the ages because of its picturesque nature, the narrow-minded stupidity of a historian who achieves popularity as a result of his stupidity, a story that becomes legendary, an image which is striking for its color. The higher the spirit climbs, the stronger this force works around it. Sometimes its action is direct. Thus, Socrates drinks the hemlock, Mani is flayed. The Albigensians are exterminated. Other times, this force acts indirectly, by burning books, as in Alexandria, or by deforming oral traditions when there are no books.

Without a doubt, the Druids of Gaul must have represented one of the highest points of spirituality that man is capable of attaining, because the force of destruction brought all of its means together against them — violence first, followed by that evasive manner of defamation which kills ideas like men.

It has been entirely successful. What remains of the ancient sages of our country? The conqueror Julius Caesar, Julius Caesar the cunning, the atheist and the heartless, who brought Roman order and the system of plundering which he called taxes to the Aedui and Allobroge peoples, managed to wrest from our Gallic ancestors their very knowledge of themselves and the degree of stature which they had achieved. After two thousand years, the Romanized children of Gaul learn in school who were the gods of Rome, while the god of the Druids remains to them unknown.

Or, rather, they have a distorted image. And that is where we see the perverse genius which has worked to erase from our consciences the religion of ancient Gaul and the lessons we could take from it. Because true spiritual heritage hides in the depths of the race and the everyday wisdom of each of us should be drawn from the wisdom of our origins.

Every young French person, whether he be taught in primary school, in high school, or in a religious institution, recognizes his ancestors by a puerile representation that the tedium of history books has transformed into an indelible cliché.

We see, on a sort of ladder, a serious figure wearing a white robe and with a long beard, facing forward. It is a Druid. His beard is removable, and is held on his face by two hooks which hang on his ears. We are reminded of award ceremonies where adolescents, wearing these badly hung beards, recited verses with a sickening banality. The Druid holds a sickle in his hand and is going to cut paper mistletoe from a cardboard oak tree. Young girls, sisters of middle school friends, stand around, smiling innocently. Behind, in the background, are young people with long moustaches, wearing rented helmets and belts. These are the Gauls. And hanging over this conventional scene is a little bit of the of the emphatic soul of Chateaubriand.

This is the childlike mental picture that everyone conjures up, almost unwittingly, upon the mention of the Gaul of the Druids and of Veleda. There is here a surprising paradox, especially when we contemplate the contrast of this image with that of the living earth of woodland plaines, marshy valleys, dense forests, with fortified, dominating cites; if we consider the indomitable people who lived in these cities and walked these valleys, and the naive and violent people, quick to change their minds, ingenuous, passing from exuberant joy to the most profound sadness; if we consider that they were guided by a mystical aristocracy of philosophers in which Pythagoras found inspiration, compared to the age when Romulus and Remus had only just sucked the milk of the she-wolf.

Primitive Gaul is deemed uninteresting, yet no Mississippi with its floating islands, no Amazon with its millions of Brazilian crocodiles, no Yangtze with its millions of Chinese birds will ever have as much vibrant life, will ever show such an outpouring of joyous nature as the Rhone where the tanned Ligurians bathed among the olive trees, as the Garonne where the Cantabrian fishers dipped their oars among giant cactuses.

Now the cactuses and the olive trees are reduced to the size of men. The descendants of the Ligurians and the Cantabrians shave their faces the Roman way, and the hair on their bodies has thinned. But what remains incomprehensible is the contempt and ignorance with which they regard the millenary spirit of their people, in favor of a Greco-Roman admiration.

To be sure, this cultural hypocrisy that each person carries within himself brings the educated Frenchman to believe that he is knowledgable of and even admires Gaul and the Druids. He will just as soon speak of the dolmens and the menhirs, which date back to several thousand years before the arrival of the Druids in Gaul. If he wishes to be honest with himself, however, he will admit that there is, like a backdrop to this knowledge, a fresco of adolescent award ceremonies, he will repeat with all the historians that the Roman conquest was fundamental to the progress of civilization, he will bow with Michelet before the genius of Julius Caesar.

Platitudes are all-powerful, and they transmit lies and injustice from epoch to epoch with ease, especially when it involves the so-called torch of civilization. Before this torch, everyone bows down. Beneath its sacrosanct light the weak are defeated by the strong and intelligent thought takes on a distorted meaning. It is passed down faithfully because there is a doctrine of banality. Its bearers are always the masters of the established order, the defenders of a law with no compassion, the possessors of a lying historical truth.

But it is fitting to impart with this same faithfulness an enduring cry of revolt.

The Roman ferocity

The breakdown of Roman society at the time of the crushing of the Gaul was perhaps even greater than the one we see in today's societies like Paris, Berlin or New-York.

Important men had no kind of faith in anything, except in satisfying their appetites. They were deeply atheists. Politicians obtained according to their influence, religious expenses, exactly like if nowadays, M. Herriot was appointed Bishop of Paris or if M. Mandel was sacred Chief Rabbi. Thus, the rude and pleaser-seeking Mark Antony, returning from the Gallic war, obtained the charge of Augur, that is to say of deciphering and inquiring heavenly things, for which he would have had a clairvoyant ascetic. Julius Caesar, in the beginning of his career, although already having a well-established reputation of an unbeliever and debaucher, obtained the position of great Pontiff by buying voters, according to Suetonius.

The then same great Roman had an unbelievable facility to pass between themselves their partners, wives, sisters or daughters, for matters of interest. It looks like their liaisons were restricted to the small circle of their relatives or well-known people. Thus Cato, who was to be for centuries the stark personification of virtue, eager to please some Hortensius, an old friend of his, who wanted his wife Marcia, hastened to repudiate her, although she was pregnant with him, gave her to Hortensius and married her again at the death of Hortensius, after this loan which lasted six years.

Between Caesar, Pompey, Cicero and Mark Antony, it is a perpetual crossover of women, a series of wedding bargaining. Sometimes, the reason being the quality of pleasure revealed by confidences made among men. But in general, it is the interest. Incest are not particularly recommended. They are commonly practiced.

Strictly speaking, such way of treating women could not be reconciled with the elevation of the soul. But it indicates that these men who were cultivated, who loved the arts and poetry, some of which had the genius of action, did not have a high conception of love and fidelity to one partner. There was also no reflection in them of the Platonic friendship of Greek philosophers. Best friends hurry assassins against each other, as soon as their interests are contrary.

The taste of Rome for monstrous things was a sign of its degeneration. There was a public market of runts where dwarfs enthusiasts went to get a supply and they were many. The great aristocratic families owned dwarves, giants, cretins, hermaphrodites, goitrous. They were brought in after meals to entertain drunkenness. One guffawed by seeing them, they were mocked and hit. Some phenomena were preserved after death. Pliny narrates that he saw corpses of dwarves in vases. In the gardens of Sallust, a vault contained bones of two famous giants, Posion and Secundilla. A female mule which put down a foal, at the time of the confusion before the battle of Pharsalia, this prodigy occupied all minds.

Another sign of degeneration was the development of gastronomy. Never at any era and at any time, had it played such a role. The habit of taking emetics to exceed the normal possibilities for human absorption is well known. It is tested by all historians. Many wealthy characters devoted themselves exclusively to food. A number of these wonderful roads, which one can still see the traces, were built only to allow certain nutrients to arrive faster to the Roman gourmets. The feasts were the main activities of daily life. They did not exclude the native coarseness of manners, since, according to Juvenal, there were two kinds of dishes, precious dishes for important people and more vulgar dishes for ordinary guests, yet served at the same table! Roman society had a love of fish that were beyond measure. A certain Gavius Apicius who had moved to Minturnae because of the quality of lobsters, travelled to African coasts to find more beautiful ones. One was brought to him when he was going to land and disgusted, he set sail without touching the ground, because they were too small!

That made men with big stomachs with faces made livid by repeated vomiting and early bare skulls. A lean senator as Cassius, who was not wearing the uniform of the overweight, was so exceptional that Julius Caesar distrusted him, seeing in him a man who was thinking too much.

World civilizers had the innate taste for political murders. Apart from gastronomy for wealthy people, politics was the main occupation of Romans. There was no election without a large number of murders. Streets offered no security. Houses either. Cicero had been forced to flee the sumptuous residence he occupied on the Palatine; a strip controlled by Antony came to destroy thoroughly this sumptuous residence and could, without interference, build a temple instead! When Cicero returned to Rome, he was forced to destroy the temple and rebuild his house.

A halo of classicism adorned falsely characters of that era. Throughout the centuries, teachers of Latin and history have put them a noble mask that hides their grimacing face of greedy men.

Cicero, whose oratorical quotes to the senseless Catiline had to be repeated by millions of college students, had a base soul. He realized the feat of being both yellow with envy and inflated by a comic vanity.

Cato was a false wise, a stoic caricature. At the time of killing himself, he speaks of Stoic philosophy and pretended to read with seriousness the dialogue on the immortality of the soul of Plato. But he gives a punch in the face of a slave with such force that he breaks in half his hand and asks a doctor to come to treat this hand, and with it he must, within hours, open his stomach.

Nothing has equaled Roman ferocity of that period. It was commonly used to file in the stands of the forum, where the speakers spoke, heads of their political enemies who had been murdered and where they were allowed to mummify.

Under Sulla, relates Florus, a certain Marcus Gratidianus, seized by a popular group, was scourged, his eyes were put out, and they cut off his hands and feet. It was only after a long wait that they cut off his head.

Catiline took this head, but the historian does not say the use he made with it.

The day of Marius's triumph, one had dragged Jugurtha, King of Numidia behind him. Scholarly torture had driven mad in advance, so that in ceremonial robes, he made extravagant gesticulations, likely to make the crowd laugh. After that, they left him for six days before strangling him, in a sewer, beneath the Capitol. It is above the cesspool that the scholar Cicero, philosopher Cicero, would look down to make sure how of their agony were Lentulus and four of his friends, he had illegally sentenced to die in this tomb.

The noble Pompey, which all historians praise the generosity, had crucified along the road from Rome to Capua, with geometric care, the six thousand companions of Spartacus he had made prisoners, so that a traveler could walk a very long time between the dead that rattled. When Cicero was put to death, his head and his cut off left hand were brought up to Antony. Immediately his wife Fulvia, pulled out the bloodless tongue and happily jabbed it with a hairpin.

It was a normal custom to expose without food in the Tiber Island, the old or sick slaves to get rid of them and a distraction, a hiking destination for large families to see them die in front of the temple of Asclepius.

It is surprising that the Romans had not scalped as the Redskins. They haven't probably thought of it. It is to these torchbearers of the spirit that was given the land of wise Druids. It is them that the millennium lie of education has taught us to admire as our intellectual fathers.

Caesar the materialist

It was said that Julius Caesar led the Roman legions in Britain only because a legend assured that in this misty land there was plenty of beads. He loved gemstones and believed in finding splendid ones in the unknown regions of the north. Perhaps the conquest of the entire Gaul had been originated by a pearl desire.

Julius Caesar is, of all famous men, the one who's genius was the less discussed. Michelet, dazzled by this genius, when he wrote the history of France has, in a manner of speaking, retracted Julius Caesar's crimes in Gaul and he exclaims:

— Such a man has no homeland. He belongs to the world.

Julius Caesar belongs only to Rome. He is its perfect, dazzling incarnation.

I do not undertake to make a portrait of Julius Caesar, nor a story of the Gallic Wars. I only want to note few details in contradiction with the universal admiration and in particular the one of Michelet.

Julius Caesar achieved to a high degree, from his youth, the type of what was known in France before the war, the cavalry officer, sportsman and seductive. He spent hours each day in the care of his toilet. His special manners made him first dubbed "the Queen of Bithynia" because of his friendship with the king of this country. He gave wide publicity to these customs, which greatly added to his prestige. But he changed after the first youth, a change that still occurs nowadays, and a taste for immoderate women came up to him, haunting, to a point that, what is wonderful in his carrier is that, he was able to satisfy this taste along with the ambitions of politician and general. He became so famous by his sexual potency that the marching song of his soldiers, jokingly called the Gallic husbands to watch over their wives, because of the presence of their leader. He also promoted this reputation of power, knowing how it was likely to lead all female hearts after him.

It must be said that he was generous, even magnificent. Maybe he was only looking for pearls as a gift for women. He gave one to Servilia, mother of Brutus, which was worth six million.

All historians are unanimous in finding him handsome. Suetonius, among his praises, mentions a fat body and a white complexion. But the many busts we have of him inspire rather repulsion. We imagine him more pallid than white. This atheist evokes a priest who would be simultaneously notary clerk. He was immensely affable, cultivated and an artist. His seduction must have come from his understanding of other people's vices, his power, of the contempt in which he held men. He suffered cruelly from his premature baldness. He brushed his latest hair forward and pretended to smooth them with his finger to ensure himself of their presence. Maybe his baldness contributed to his hatred of the Gauls, too hairy in his opinion. He had to see with satisfaction the merchants who followed the legions, cut the long hair of the dead so that they might serve as false braids to the Roman ladies.

His frankness was extolled because he did not hesitate to be cynical. But the greatest hypocrisy is the one which affects the cynicism. His taste for luxury was such that he couldn't do without having a floor in his room in a wood marquetry, and at war, he had this wood brought to his suite and had the floor of the rooms where he slept change. This did not prevent him from detracting luxury in Rome by banning the use of litters, purple and even wearing pearls which was allowed only to certain people!

He blames the Druids, on the basis of gossip made by defectors, to perform blood sacrifices, he who, besides the carnage of war, killed for his pleasure and that of the rabble he flattered, thousands of gladiators.

The quality of irony about it should be noted. After telling about the extermination of the inhabitants of the city of Cenabum, he also said:
—Little had to be regretted.

He had the ability to forgive often to political enemies, killing the practitioner only for material benefits and not for revenge, over which he placed himself. This is what made his reputation of magnanimity. Perhaps he was not cruel in the ordinary sense. A man who has sexual pleasure perpetually in his disposition, feel that he has no time to lose in seeking revenge. He had an abstract cruelty, a transcendent faculty of extermination, beyond imagination. It must have been very great for after the account of his cruelties in Gaul, there were senators to propose to hand him over, bound hand and foot to the Gauls. It is true that this proposal was greeted with laughter.

After taking Uxellodunum, in the Lot, he had cut off the right wrist to a thousand warriors who came to visit him, naively trusting his generosity. The author of the comments adds:

"Caesar, who knew that his goodness was known to all and had no fear that an act of force was charged to the cruelty of his character determined to make an example."[1]

He signed a treaty of peace with the Usipete and the German Tencteri and taking advantage of the fact that they were unarmed, he immediately made an unprecedented massacre.

Great military genius! was cried out.

This politician warrior and man of the world, kept for six years in the Capitol underground sewers, the loyal Vercingetorix who had visited him. He made him strangle the night of the ceremony of his triumph, and later between the torches, he had marched among animals and stolen objects.

This women expert made also march in this triumph, the young Arsinoe of Egypt. A giraffe pranced behind her. A sign bearded in huge letters: *Veni, Vidi, Vixi*, terms of a letter of Caesar to his friend Amantius whom his fans had made famous.

Can we imagine such a foolish vanity for a general to include in a procession a fortunate sentence of his correspondence!

He fell into an even greater complacency. The love of a true queen, Cleopatra, had almost made him lose his mind. Like the pettiest bourgeois of our republics, he falsified his genealogy, he claimed to descent from Aeneas and even the goddess Venus!

All these features have not prevented the posterity of thinking he was sublime because he succeeded. He has extended over Gaul the power

1 Translation Maurice Rat (Garnier).

of his destructive intelligence. If there are missionaries of evil - and the mission is ignored even by the one who accomplishes it - Caesar was one them. Annihilating his forces, he turned Gaul towards the material civilization of Rome. He killed the spirit and gave in exchange roads, monuments, circuses. Those he had left to live were satisfied. The Gauls appreciated the conveniences of the central hitting and the Roman baths. They pride themselves on having representatives in the senate of Rome and their best horsemen enrolled themselves under the orders of Mark Antony. Caesar's name was glorified such as one of the great civilizers of humanity.

However, if there are some who believe that an inner clockwork of justice, hidden in the equity structure, go off with the production of evil, they will be happy to think that, Julius Caesar could not give to any queen, the pearls of India he dreamed of conquering and that he was killed by his own son, the only person he possibly loved.

The Swastika

Historians speak about Forgotten peoples which probably had occupied Gaul before any invasion, Aryan, at the time origins[1].

Forgotten peoples! It is impossible to resist to the magical evocation of these words. We see crystal beaches off when standing in the midst, men with blue eyes looking in the horizon of veiled seas, the contours of the fabulous Ireland. We represent ourselves virgins with braided hair who set out annually through the vast western and went carrying wheat in the temple of Delos. We imagine them building these graves and the burial crypts so that their dead rest in peace in the silence of underground rocks.

History cannot set exact dates for the coming of successive races.

Celts, Galatians, Ligurians, Aquitani, had in turn occupied Gaul and there were mingled with the Forgotten men. Then came the Druids, but one could not determine more, neither at what time nor from what region they left.

In the entire France were found, on stones of great antiquity, the swastika, which is par excellence the sign of the religion of India, the primitive solar symbol. Its place on steles, on altars and in sanctuaries, indicates that it was the object of a cult. It is especially in the south of France and in some valleys of the Pyrenees as the valley of Larboust that were found swastikas. The reason of it is perhaps that in those places less exposed to invasions, tribes which inhabited had more leisure to receive the first seed of eternal thought.

Educated men in olden days summarized their science in signs and these signs had several meanings, depending on the degree of knowledge of those who interpreted them. Swastika signified the power of time and when it became a purely Buddhist sign, he symbolized the

1 They were of Turanian race, according to M. Alexandre Bertrand. (*La religion des Gaulois.*)

wheel of life to which men is bound and of which he manages to free himself only by purification. Nowadays, its meaning has been completely transformed since in Germany it means hatred of races and desire for violence. But in earlier ages, where simple and pious men engraved the Swastika on the stones of the Gauls, it was only synonymous of good omen, of pure light and eternal salvation.

Swastikas were brought into Gaul by the Druids. The Druids did not come to teach a religion and the cult of some Gods, but a philosophy of the world. That is why they did not offer to the veneration of men neither Jupiter, nor an Osiris, nor a Teutates with a face and a human body, but a sign that contained an idea and where everyone could find a spiritual nutrient, according on its level of understanding.

The Druids did not leave monuments of their thinking. The principle of their ancient knowledge was that all education should be oral. If, however, they had left a written testimony, it is likely that the Christian leveling would have destroyed these detestable remnants of paganism.

They were unknown to an unconceivable point. The most detailed information we have on them come from the comments of Julius Caesar who, not only did he not know them but, was of all men, the one who had the most interest to deny their superiority.

Julius Caesar had known only one Druid, the Aedui Diviciacus, and it is from him that he kept his vague knowledge of Druidry. Cicero, who speaks of the Druids with contempt and who considers the Gauls as primitive people, also says[1]:

— I have known a Druid, the Aedui Diviciacus.

And he told that this Diviciacus who came in Italy with Julius Caesar spoke in the Roman curia, leaning on his shield.

Yet, this unique Druid has given on the internal organization of Druidry only the most general information, those the last slave knew because he was probably a false Druid. He adorned himself with this title to suggest a secret power over the Gallic tribes of the north and obtain the support of the Roman legions against the Allobroges, with who the Aedui were at war. He reached his ends by his intrigues. His

1 Cicero: *De Republica*

goal was even surpassed. He had to become for future historians, the ultimate Druid. The fact that a priest, traveling in a warrior costume and wearing a shield to give an acceptance speech to the Roman senate, did not appear shocking to anyone. M. Camille Jullian, in his *Histoire des Gaules*, will even naively assume that he might have been "The great pontiff of Gauls."

Julius Caesar had to justify in the eyes of the Roman people, the destruction of cities, the massacre of inhabitants, the devastation of countries. It was necessary, to some extent, to explain the mood that had been his, near the defensive walls on fire of Uxellodunum, before the severed hands of men of the Lot whose piles had to have a certain height. Mysterious mood, moreover, of an army general after a victory and which is hard to imagine.

And that is why he wrote about the Druids, what he considered as a justification. It was a bit like if Warren Hastings, first Governor of India, after the repression of Benares, have had to write a recall on Vedanta philosophy. He would have spoken, according to the language of the missionaries, of pagan idols and of the uncleanliness of ascetics.

Julius Caesar drew a rough image, a puerile tableau, likely to impress all souls, those of virtuous senators and those of mothers of legionaries. According to him, human sacrifices were a public institution in Gaul. The people whose fortified cities he had shaved and destroyed populations, were miserable people enslaved to a monstrous clergy who had found and who practiced the rites of the ancient Moloch. The serial novel did not yet exist but Caesar has already found its popular color that seduces by its mystery. The Druids were all the more horrible as they were invisible. They formed a secret society, a Ku Klux Clan who was hiding in the darkness of forests.

"Some have manikins of an enormous size they fill with living men the wicker shell. One puts it on fire and men perish, enveloped by the flame[1]."

He alleviates well this tableau by saying that only criminals were used for those holocausts. But it is in order to cry out hypocritically:

1 Translation Maurice Rat (Garnier).

"One comes to sacrifice even innocents!"

Pliny, Diodorus, Strabo repeated what he had said. There is no wonder that a century after the Gallic Wars, one was misinformed about the customs and the civilization of this part of the West. With all our actual information means, little is known and we do not want to know how Europe's armies destroyed in 1860, monuments and libraries of China for example. It takes a long curve of centuries to see appear this weak justice of the reprobation of cultivated men is. But what is surprising is that so many centuries have passed and that Julius Caesar, on the faith of his warrior spirit, could impose this postcard, this chromo representing a manikin where there are men in it burning, and all around it, Druids with sickles. What is surprising is that a historian like M. Camille Jullian could go on about the text of the Comments and add to the manikin of wood and hay:

"The convicts were confined pell-mell with animals in a huge wicker manikin of wood and hay and fire was put to this mass of flesh."

Human sacrifices that have been so much alleged to Gauls and to Druids existed in all times and among all peoples. Nowadays, only few nations only have abolished them. France is not one of them. Only the sacrifice instead of being made with a sacred knife, is practiced by the guillotine and it is not in the name of Moloch, of Jupiter or of Teutates, but in the name of an abstract deity of justice.

These sacrifices which outraged so much Julius Caesar were still practiced frequently of his time, in some regions of the Roman Empire. They were still made in the 11th century AD in Arcadia and in a much later period, the free Roman people, the civilizing people had to use, when a public emergency threatened the city, to bury alive in the Forum Boarium, a Gaul and a Gaulish woman, despite the obvious lack of connection between this torture and the march of destiny.

After a million men had been slaughtered, one million is the figure given by Plutarch, Gaul was considered pacified. It was concluded that the absence of uprisings meant the satisfaction of having received the blessings of civilization. All peoples are pacified when their assets have been exterminated and there is no one to speak out against the exterminators.

Rome sent prefects, officials and especially tax collectors. All, when they returned, spoke in a low voice of those deep forests they had coasted by going to their posts and where, here and there, were still accomplished some human sacrifices. Perhaps there was some who have heard the cry of the victims.

But no one stopped at the edge of the road, before some ancient stone stele of which a milestone had been made, to consider the meaning of this incomprehensible sign that came from a distant past, this mysterious wheel, the swastika[1].

---

1 It has been given different interpretations of the Swastika. Burnouf has made it the symbol of fire, Max Muller of the sun, G. Alviella that of the moon, Miss Blavatsky that of the initiatory center of the world; René Guenon has made it the sign of the Pole. In ancient India this sign symbolized the movement accomplished in joy, life in march toward perfection. This is the most likely meaning for a sign that was placed on the threshold of all the temples and in all intersections.

The druidic lamaseries

It is unknown in what era the Druids came to Gaul. We only know that they appeared, stayed a few centuries and then disappeared. But to understand the enigmatic character of their arrival and the few material traces they left of their presence, we should be aware that, in all times, in the entire world, there has been wandering communities, depositaries of human knowledge. At all times, these communities have proceeded by the same methods, strove toward the same goal and had the common rule to remain hidden.

The fist character of thought is to be visible. Many travellers passed through India and Tibet and had only seen miserable populations, indulging in childish superstitions. The lector of the Vedas and of the Bhagavad Gita does not stand, book in hand, on the passage of the caravan. Moreover, if we imply a creature of another planet looking at Paris from afar, this creature would realize than men move, eat and get closer for love, but it would not realize that they think. This is what happens, furthermore, for the observer of an ant society. He cannot distinguish if among the warriors, the layers and the other small specialized creatures are wise metaphysicians.

There have always been men who possessed essential truths which allow humanity to move confusedly towards an ideal of perfection. And these men have transported themselves across the world to teach these truths, seek other men, among the most advanced and most eager of culture, so that these truths are perpetuated.

From where, originally, have these missionaries travelers started from? Various explanations had been given, many of which have a wonderful character and ask to add faith to know some legends.

The most marvelous hypothesis is the one which gives them a divine origin. Some occultists claim that beings, who have reached a greater development than ours and inhabiting the Venus planet, would have sent messengers on earth to give men the foundations of knowledge. These messengers would have instructed disciples who, in turn, would have passed the knowledge on to others.

Everyone now knows the Agartha and the king of the world of who spoke Ossendowski. Saint Yves d'Alveydre, noble and emphatic writer, in a book entitled *Mission de l'Inde*, claimed to have had a revelation that Agartha and the king of the world, his leader, had a real and active life, but underground. It would be in the shadows of the center of the earth that would develop the spiritual forces which govern us.

Mr. René Guenon wrote on this topic a very complete and definitive book[1] in which he brings all the eastern and western traditions, for Agartha, the Manu of the Hindus and to this mysterious land, "sacred island", or "Mount of salvation" whose traditions of all peoples make an insider stay. Mr. René Guenon tends to conclude that the Agartha and the "land of Immortality" will not always be invisible to men. They are so, only because we are in the Kali Yuga or period of obscuration. But a time will come when insiders will reappear and when the aim will cease to be hidden.

A tradition which affects the one of Agartha is the one which states that after the great cosmic disaster where Atlantis was swallowed, there were men who escaped and gave themselves the task of perpetuating the human moral heritage. They took refuge on the heights of the Himalayas. There, they buried the astronomical tables, documents engraved on sheets of metal, all that represented the elements of knowledge. It is from there that they left again across the world which became barbaric again.

The legendary character of these traditions is radiant. We can also suppose that, in a natural way and without any watchword, the most cultivated men have gathered in an attempt to make humanity less rude with purer manners and a broader knowledge.

But it is necessary to note that these groups, which are emerging from the most remote times, all have had the same discipline, the same way

1 René Guenon: *Le Roi du Monde.*

of living and have taught the same science.

They come in the form of communities that have several degrees, according to the tendency of their members. These communities live in a secluded way, they practice certain asceticism, and they do not aspire to speak of them. They do not build great monuments, so that when they disappear, their existence is easily denied. They have for principle that the greatest influence is of spiritual nature and that to practice it, nor stone tower nor armed sergeants are needed.

The magus of Chaldea, the Orphic groups of Greece, the Essenes of Palestine, the Pythagoreans, the Therapeutae of Egypt, the Druids in Gaul were communities of that order. There must have been others that we ignore, because of their deliberate bias not to leave tracks.

It is through their everywhere existence, thanks to the Freemasonry of knowledge, that men eager to learn were welcomed in the most distant countries. Having only his coat and his staff, the one who was born under the star of knowledge, found, from India to Ireland, whatever the savagery of peoples, places of wisdom and education, where he was given a password that allowed him to go further. Thus, Pythagoras is said to have been in India and among the Druids of Gaul. It was shown for a long time in Memphis, the room where Plato had lived. Apollonius of Tyana and Manes, traveled the east and west and visited all the places where there was an education to receive. Few years ago, the Russian Nicolas Notovitch found in the Buddhist monastery of Hinis, in Tibet, the track of the stay made there by Jesus[1].

These wandering communities had a religious character, since the first principles of their beliefs were the unity of God and the immortality of the soul. But when they settled in a country, they were not trying to turn people away from their cult, they complied to it, certain that the truths that they possessed the secrets would not fail to filter among the most intelligent. They were well greeted everywhere, because they generally taught new processes to work iron, make pottery and knowledge for the construction of bridges and buildings. They altered according to races, the tone of their teaching. Thus, the magus of Chaldea became priests

1 N.Notovitch: *La Vie inconnue de Jésus Christ.*

of an astronomical religion. The Orphic Greece founded the mysteries. The Essenes developed doctrines of brotherhood and love of the poverty which Jesus had to make public. Maybe there were Chinese communities to spread a morality of life to the use of agricultural populations, whose dream did not exceed the rice field and the tombstone of the ancestors.

Druids probably left from a centre located in Irelànd, center that originally had to supply in Asia, as the close similarity of organization of the Druids and Lamas proves it.

They found in Gaul, Celtic gods called Teutates, Esus, Taranis[1], and those countless demons that haunt the surface of the earth and which have in turn been called devas, daemons, fairies or angels.

They respected these gods like they respected the dolmens and the standing stones that stood on Armoricans trays, on the plains of centre and south. The Druids had nothing to do with, like it is commonly thought, the elevation of dolmens and standing stones. These stones date back to much earlier times perhaps those of Atlantis. Dolmens were tombstones that rain have developed, while standing stones were erected to summon the spirits, and ease their communications with men. Standing stones were meeting points of celestial spirits. One can suppose that many dolmens were still underground at the time when the Druids came to Gaul and yet three thousand years of rain were needed to make appear the bones of forgotten leaders who were resting under their vaults.

Moreover, there are dolmens nearly everywhere on the surface of the planet. "Thus, William Gowland have explored, measured, photographed, four hundred and six of them in Japan, some thirty years ago[2]." They were consequently built by races which had common ideas on construction and on death and which were widespread in all the countries. The Druids used them, as well as Christianity had to use them later.

A very curious thing reported by Mr. Chaboseau, there is a sea-green

1 The importance of these Gods is uncertain. They are only mentioned by the poet Lucain. On the basis of this single poet, all historians have identified them as the three major Gods of Gaul. These historians have forgotten how easily the poets throw to haphazard proper sonorous nouns in their poems.

2 A. Chaboseau: *Histoire de la Bretagne avant le XIIIe siècle.*

gemstone, similar to turquoise, the callaïs, which we know only 830 pearls in the world, all of which have been found in the dolmens.

What virtue had this rare gemstone, what virtue of a mortuary use and what possibilities for the future life were hidden in it? This opens a great flight to the imagination at which no answer might be given.

Like Essenes in Palestine, the Druids did not find themselves in the presence of an organized and closed clergy. They conquered immediately the welcoming and naive race that lived along the Loire and the Garonne in this former Gaul which cannot more simply be described as by that phrase so evocative of Diodorus of Sicily:

"Gaul is crossed by large and numerous rivers which weave through the plains. Some are rooted in deep lakes and other spring from the mountains."

According to the immutable method of spiritual communities of those distant times, some of them became active educators, became judges, builders and doctors, whereas the others devoted themselves to the study of the stars, taught philosophy and the journey of the soul after death.

Like Mr. A. Bertrand[1] demonstrated it in his book *La religion des Gaulois*, the inner part of the Druids group led a cloistered life in monasteries, in lamaseries, organized like the current lamaseries in Tibet. The primitive model remained immutable on the slopes of the Himalayas protector, from where went the theories of the first messengers, where many isolated from the minds attempt to return, even today, who consider themselves as lonely messengers.

The Druids founded the monastic life in the west. It is on their organization that formed later Christian monasteries and abbeys of the first centuries after Jesus Christ. As well as on the vast arid plateaus of Mongolia and Tibet, among still savage populations, are located like small islands, monasteries with libraries and spiritual practices, likewise

---

1 *La Religion des Gaulois*, by Mr. A. Bertrand, member of the Institute, summarizes the course that made the author at the school of Louvre in 1896. I am giving these titles for those who might ignore the name of Mr. A. Bertrand and might not believe in his authority. It should be noted that, when a book is revealing, on any matter, it rarely becomes famous and it is the humdrum books, mulling over the old false perceptions that have all the popularity.

there were among Gallic lands of vast forests, and up to the narrow gorg-
es of the Pyrenees, colleges of educated men, holders of art and science.
The historian Strabo described the life of one of these communities at
Comona in Asia Minor. This one had acquired in its time, in the first
part of the first century, great prosperity and influence. It had become
a commercial center as well as a spiritual one. The number of its members amounted to more than six thousand. A town was built nearby. The
territory of the community had such a sacred character that the barbarian invasions plundered the area but did not touch Comona. Same
reasons produce same effects. Druid's lamaseries, like those of Tibet
or the one of Comona, formed oases of thought, among still primitive
peoples. They "possessed hereditary secrets of crafts and national traditions", they draw up maps of countries for travelers, taught those who
were eager for knowledge, the spherical shape of the earth, movement
of planets and the symbols hidden behind the emblematic representations of Gods. They also taught a higher philosophy to those who were
likely to understand it. This philosophy could be called the perennial
philosophy, since it is found, with only slight variations, among the early
initiators of human taught. We will see that the Druids have marked
this philosophy with the seal of their own wisdom."

The Hindu mother and the Gallic mothers

There is in India a goddess all men invoke at certain hours, whatever the sect they belong to. This is the Mother. It is her that Hindu poems call the goddess with a dark blue complexion, the one that embodies the forces of nature, beauty and death, the one that leads to the divine absolute, by the path of enthusiasm. It is to her that prayed Rama Krishna in Benares, in the temple with five domes, of the whispers of the Ganges waters, and cymbal that the servants made resonate. It is while kneeling in front of these invisible symbols, that he saw, one evening, coming to him an "Ocean of mind", he was covered by these immense waves at the same time as he was touched by the feeling of a divine presence.

The Mother is everywhere. Everywhere, the ocean of mind is hidden and it hurries if one breaks some inner dikes. The Mother symbolizes the realization of the ideal beauty. In the admiration of beauty, whether that of a woman walking or that of a tree that springs to a height, the man reaches an intermediary state between intuition and intelligence. This state is the highest summit where the men's mind can get.

The Mother has always been represented with a feminine shape. Christians give her the name of Virgin Mary. But when they brought the cult of the Virgin Mary to Gaul, there was no Gaul who did not already knew her. They only called her differently for centuries. And as the mother presented to them under the infinite diversity of living forms of nature, she was for them, the Mothers.

These goddesses were countless and they applied a daily protective action. There was one in every fountain, in every rock forming a shelter, in every tree, more majestic and more ancient than the other trees in the woods. There were Mothers of the house and family Mothers. The Gauls, who were fighting far from home, were accompanied by a personal Mother who linked them to the distant home and whose protection they felt. Each fountain was the expression in matter of a living Mother and lots of them accomplished miraculous healings with their waters.

Earth, waters and woods were animated for Gauls by a mysterious divine life. There were hidden spirits, geniuses and Mothers everywhere. Some places were more conducive than others to the presence of deities. One went there then on pilgrimage, stone enclosures were raised around it and fires were lit there before daybreak.

Christianity, whilst fighting the pagan errors, had enough empowerment to take advantage of their powers. Many churches were built on places which have been haunted by ancient Mothers. Many miraculous fountains were sanctified and ladies or saints replaced goddesses of olden times.

Chartres's Cathedral is built on the ancient sanctuary of Autricum, capital of Carmutes. In the eighteenth century, in the choir of Notre-Dame, was found a stone bearing an image of Esus and an image of Jupiter which shows that the location of the Christian cathedral had been, in earlier times, the location of a temple to primitive gods.

Near the Garonne, in Toulouse, was located a sacred place whose power was immemorial. The Romans built there a temple, and the Visigoths, a Christian church. This church is today called the Daurade, and was, originally, dedicated to the Virgin Mary, that is to say, to the Mother. Only owls' heads on the columns confirms that the goddess, who, in the primitive times, blew his inspirations with the voice avec the Pyrenean waters and tall poplars, was the goddess of the clear-sighted intelligence, who had as a symbol the bird that sees through the night.

It is the same for the Maison Carrée of Nîmes, the Montmorillon octagonal temple in Poitou and many local churches and chapels erected on hills or in valleys where the spirit blew in all times because he wanted to blow there.

Mothers have lived there in olden days. They have only change names. But they hear the calls formulated with other syllables by men of the same race. They are still hidden under the stones of Christian altars. And when a believer whispers: Hail Mary! It is Onuava that stands between the altar candles and whispers: I am here.

The Druids taught that the statues are vain and that we should not draw representations of Gods because of the ease with which simple men take the matter symbolizing the mind, for the mind himself. Most of the statues that were erected despite them, have been destroyed by Christians, eager to destroy all vestige of paganism. Scarcely had remained here and there, some forgotten statuettes or some low reliefs on a monument.

The most striking image of Gallic Goddesses is the one to which we give the goddess name of Onuava and that archaeologists who speak of her, call "kind of Minerva" or celestial Venus.

The Onuava goddess, found on an old hospital door in Clermont, keeps this beauty the sculptor of olden days tried to put on her face and which the wear and tear of the stone could not erase the soul. She participates in the fluidity of waters because she has fish scales on her ears. Two snakes are deploying around her, two snakes with bird heads, which are the symbols of knowledge and wisdom by which it was prescribed to man, from the beginning of time, to make its way towards perfection. Of his brain come out two wings, emblems of the flight, of ideal aspiration, of the uplift of the physical world, to reach the most perfect world of the mind.

This intangible nature of the goddess Onuava, was reconciled with nature, purely terrestrial in appearance, of the Gallic Mothers.

For there are two meanings behind the face of all deities. Under the appearances of the physical nature, under the gushing waters of the earth, under the pressure of plant sap, in carnal forms swollen with blood, there is the force that aspires to return to its source. One flourishes in beauty, the other changes this beauty into mind. Mothers were the symbols of these two forces. Druids penetrated the secret of Mothers. They knew that behind the manifestations of nature, terrestrial or celestial, were hiding presences and that behind these presences were the essences of the world. The Druids were the priests of the cult of the Mothers.

The death of forests

As the Gauls were hairy with river-colored eyes, and the land that engendered them, was recovered with thick forests, cut off by the lines of the waters of the French Riviera.

Gaul did not look like our country. The living side of a region takes another aspect with the passage of centuries. Gaul was the kingdom of plants and the race of men was prone to trees. Men worshiped those powerful, ancient trees, constantly engendered by the substance of their bodies. They drew their life of these benevolent gods; they communicated with their materialized souls; they built their cities in accordance with the societies that formed huge forests; they were dependent on herbal kings and in this state of simplicity, they found happiness.

It is with the Roman invasion that began in Gaul, the war of trees against men and the so-called civilization to which a planetary law gives eternal victory. It is already striking to think about the death of the verdant giants and their burial in geological turmoil that preceded the known periods of history. There are trees cemeteries. It was found in the coalfields of the Autun basin, immense forests of burials. At a time that we cannot set, during unimaginable cosmic storms, under a sun that the Jurassic mist made maybe even bigger, they were swallowed up with their parasites, their wild beasts and birds. In the bay of Saint-Brieuc, along the coast of the Finistère and also in the sea which separates Ireland from England, one knows that there are large areas of petrified wood that rest under the marine vases and whose mineralized branches are now grazed by depths fish.

But the destruction of nature by itself is only a form of its rebirth. More painful is the destruction of a reign, by another.

At the time of the Druids, forests extended continuously from Ireland to the Mediterranean. Vegetable fortresses erected on both shores of the Channel. Rivers made their way by rolling trunks that blocked the mouths. Gallic roads were struggling to survive. The strength of invasion of trees would long remain, since we have found in Flanders, paved Roman roads which had in turn disappeared under the pressure of trees. Many vegetations of that period left the earth where their tree-shaped relatives were killed. Thus, the coasts of the Mediterranean from Nice to Saint-Raphaël were covered by an impenetrable forest of ash trees. This forest survived few more centuries since we see it in the tenth century, used as a rampart by its density against the Moors invasions. His recollection remains only in the names of some villages. The old ash trees are dead and have already been replaced by trees, some of which are from Arab importation, like myrtle and orange trees. Tree breeds are changing their place of residence, like the races of men.

"While boarding on the coast of Massilia, the Roman penetrated into our country and while moving forward towards the north, he encountered increasingly thick woods, more and more extensive[1]." Chestnut trees covered the central plateau and the alders the country of the Arverni. Poplars and cypresses were already standing on the hills, between Narbonne and Toulouse. The pines stretched by millions on Aquitaine dunes. The oaks were everywhere.

It is of one of the forests located in Marseille's surroundings that Lucan made such terrible description, that it is pleasant. Perhaps this description was only a poetic fantasy for him. But all historians have naively taken it seriously.

"Here are celebrated dreadful Druidic mysteries, he said. All trees are disgusting by the blood of human victims. The flowing water is black. A monstrous snake wraps to each oak tree."

Lucan still reports that when Caesar ordered to its legionaries to cut the trees of this forest, they refused, impressed by the majesty which emanated from them. Caesar the atheist was forced to grasp an ax and to strike the first blow, to show them that there was no hellish vengeance to fear.

He must have felt, by accomplishing this gesture, that he was attacking an enemy as impressive as the riders of Vercingetorix. It was then that

1 Alfred Maury: *Histoire des grandes forêts de la Gaule.*

started the extermination of trees. The forests attacked by ax and fire are quickly destroyed. For the conquered country would give its maximum output, many roads and cultivated planes were needed. The Gauls, like all peoples, found that there was benefit to change a primitive existence, whose deep richness remains invisible, against a life where welfare is visible, which is embellished by the variety of products, the choice of fabrics and more comfortable houses. They collaborated in destroying the forest dwellings of the gods. From the country of the Aedui along the Moselle, to that of Aquitaine, along the Pyrenees, fires blazed, fires that were lit for a century. The lands that were cultivated at the moment of the arrival of Caesar's legions were sufficient enough for the needs of the Gauls. It was necessary that the extent of these lands was multiplied to suffice the requirements of the conquerors. Rome, the Rome of the idle gastronomes, pot-bellied politicians, was like the enormous stomach of the empire, tirelessly absorbing the products of enslaved peoples. A century is enough to stop the vegetal development of the hairy Gaul. And already under Tiberius, wise proconsuls who had income of forests as well as fields, were forced to make edicts to prevent excessive deforestation.

But the great Gallic forests have been stroke to death. They were like a quartered man, tortured, amputated, to whom only one part of its members remains. Large smooth trunks had come down the rivers to be shipped to Massilia or in Fréjus; they journeyed to Italy by the southern routes. In losing its forests, the stripped Gaul was going to change of spirit.

Since then, French historians have recounted, sometimes with sadness, the defeat of Versingetorix at Alesia. Some have considered that the Roman victory was a happy necessity, always in virtue of this civilizing torch of which the Romans were supposed to enlighten the world. But no one has mentioned the importance of Caesar's symbolic gesture, striking a tree, no one has thought of associating the defeat of men to the defeat of forests.

The pact with nature

The Druids had made an alliance pact with forests. It corresponded then to a reality because forests were alive. What nowadays is seen as superstition and legend was a truth three thousand years ago. Tree spirits, geniuses of nature existed when their earthly bodies had not been maimed.

Now, they are not visible to the destructive race of creatures with two legs, which puts all his pleasure in making them die. They know that the most innocent girl of men will only think of, while going to places they live in, tearing off what they have created with love and what is their adoration, the flowers.

At the time when forests were silent and where the vegetation blossomed freely, the living essence of trees materialized and could become visible for some men who reached the foresight of the more subtle world that surrounds us. All primitive men speak of these shy, fleeting and benevolent creatures, which are the spirits of nature and all ascribe them the same qualities and the same defects, because they may have had of them the same experience.

Nymphs, dryads and fairies are the same beings. But we have become accustomed to consider them as purely mythological. We have heard about so many fantastic stories about fairies, they are so closely associated with childish and unbelievable tales, that we cannot venture the hypothesis of their real existence without raising a laughter.

In the old times, this existence was no doubt to anyone. The Christian church in its first effort to convert the world, encountered the deities of nature that were everywhere, under the shadows of all woods, in the blue of all sources. It didn't thought then, to deny their existence, because it was an impossibility. If there had been cultivated persons for not to believe in spirits of nature, the church would had relied on their opinion. But there was none and it was forced to declare that all deities of trees and waters were demons, animated by the evil force.

It is possible that a category of beings which still had, two thousand years ago, a real and visible existence, has now disappeared, either because it had been extinguished or because it took refuge in more inaccessible places. The existence of these beings is not unlikely. There is a collective green soul. Why should there not be special souls of species and individuals? Why these souls should not take a materialized form which under certain influences, would be perceived by some men. This is no surprise that this form affects the human form. The man being the most complicated being of the creation and the only one who have developed a consciousness, it is his form that is normally the confusing ideal of all lives which embraced in a community, tend to a particular existence.

And also the spirits of nature, one should call more precisely the souls of nature, take on the appearance of men they used to see. The legends represent the Kobold, wearing a brown cloth, with a hood, similar to the costumes of the peasants of Middle Ages. Fairies appear as the young girl of the village, or that of the castle. If any soul of tree, overcoming its timid nature, dared today to leave its bark envelope, it would probably have gloves and motorist glasses.

The souls of the trees were, in very rare cases, seen and studied by clairvoyants. They take, in virtue of unknown reasons, men and women appearances in turn. They are gifted with a plastic processing power, with the ability to contract and to spread. They possess a gift of half-luminosity of twilight color, with which in the night, ascribed to their translucent form, has a character of moving mystery for the ignorant man. The vitality of the tree with which they merge partially, form a magnetic system that protects them and which is their substance.

The legends are always referring to woodland fairy dances or gnomes of the earth. All those to whom it was allowed to see the spirits of nature are unanimous in saying that they are of joyous nature. Nature accomplishes its work in joy, and this joy dominates as awareness grows in the higher realms. The sprouts and blooms are works of joy. Roots penetration, saps rising, leafs thrust are felt emotionally by the soul of the tree as an expansion of happiness and that happiness has a communication property, it can be transmitted to the man if he can find a point of contact between the vegetable happiness and his own heart.

It is this secret that the Druids possessed. Large Gallic forests were their allies, it is from them that they drew their strength. The essential rule of the Druids was not to destroy anything that lives, a rule that also had the Pythagoreans, the Essenes, and all major brotherhoods of ancient sages. That is why nowhere were found monuments that served as homes for Druids. It would have required cutting down forests for seating or columns and their principle was to respect them. Druids lived under the arches of trees in small dwellings of which only one season was necessary to erase the traces. It is in the forests they held their colleges where they attracted young Gauls eager to learn and where the course of study lasted twenty years.

We have no idea of the science of the Druids which was transmitted orally. The naturalist Pliny made a description of a Druidic ceremony on the mistletoe gathering. This description must have had an extraordinary fortune, a fortune it does not deserve. Thanks to Pliny, it is fixed forever in the memory of men and no one can talk about Druid without mentioning mistletoe.

However it should be remembered how easily Pliny could tell picturesque details on countries that were unknown to him. What he says, for example about horned ants of India, cause one to question the other details he gives about things he could not see.

"This ant draws gold from caves. It has the color of the cat and the size of the wolf of Egypt. The gold it draws in winter is stolen by the Indians during the heat of summer. Then, they run and tear thieves up while they run away on very fast camels, so great is their agility, combined with their passion for gold."[1]

The mistletoe however, must have played a role in the preparation of the sacred beverage of the Druids. Emblem of the oak-tree, it contained the favorable strength of this tree. Thanks to a preparation which Druids had the secret, it was used to transmit to men benevolence, peace of

1 *PLIME*: book XL

mind, essential qualities of forests and especially oak forests.

This is where the main role of Druids was, their means of influencing Gallic people. They communicated with the major vegetable forces of forests. The souls of the trees are severe and gentle, they have the serenity that is the substance of the joy of living. The Druids were the agents of transmission between forests and men.

No text says it. It is engraved on no stone. But this is a time when writing was not in use. The Druids gave to the simple people of the Gauls, the life lesson of forests. They had taught them the kind of happiness that was most accessible to them. They kept them in an upright life and pure morals that are the first conditions to be happy. They fashioned their souls in accordance with the joy of expression of trees.

When Caesar entered Gaul, it has not been a long time that the case of Bacchanalia had pointed out in Rome, the organization of a large society of debauchery such as the world has ever know. Under the pretext of religious rites, the young women and the sons of the most important figures of the society, practiced certain nights, love in common, in huge proportions, since these meetings of an orgiastic character included several thousand people. This use was not lost in the time of Caesar, it had only become more secret. It even had to expand with the growing atheism of the society.

Following the legionaries, merchants who accompanied the armies, countless official parasites, the Roman louse spread in Gaul. Yet, for an inexplicable phenomenon, the corruption of morals and all evils it engenders, apply on simple and attractive peoples, an attractive seduction to which they have never resisted.

The essential wisdom

Posidonius, a Stoic philosopher of Rhodes, still living in the time of Caesar and Cicero, came to Marseille, as one goes to the world's end, to learn about the customs of primitive peoples. He knew the Gauls by these Greek merchants, cunning and greedy men who hated men of forests because of their good faith, their ingenuousness and the difficulty they had to make them accept gold and silver coins, in exchange for products of their country. The Gauls, when Posidonius came to Marseilles, a century before Christ, still did not understand why some metals, to which was given a circular shape, were sought by men.

This Posidonius, who instructed in Rome, had the Greco-Latin culture of that time, a culture that had examined the religions from all sides and concluded, in the philosophical field, to a sort of atheism based on human reason. He was himself a mathematician and politician and he understood nothing of what he could learn from the philosophy of the Druids.

Friend of Cicero and Pompey, he made these great handlers of men laugh, by talking to them about this people who had long despised gold. He wrote about the religion of Druids, in works that are lost and his opinion has fuelled all writers that followed. Thus, the Druids were known in the universe, through two sceptics, a talker and a soldier, also unfit to be affected by their wisdom.

It is what is unimportant which is spread more easily. That the Druids have had several classes, Vates, soothsayers, bards, and they had been under the authority of a great Pontiff they elected, was repeated over and over again through the centuries. What is important to remember is that all historians of antiquity, Strabo, Pliny, Diogenes, Laertes, Lamblichus and after them the church fathers, gave the Druids unanimously the highest title in order of thinking, the title of philosophers.

At the top of their hierarchy composed of poets, judges and moral counsellors, and which also had to include all clergy, impostors, there was a steering group of scientists and philosophers, who transmitted the secrets of science and metaphysical. Twenty years of study were needed to get to cross the last degree of the hierarchy of wisdom. And the revelation of what was learned was forbidden on penalty of death.

But no one thought of betraying the secrets of which one had been instructed. Divitiac himself, the so-called shield Druid who was Caesar's companion, revealed nothing to the conqueror, nothing he was at least able to understand. It is true that maybe he knew nothing. Like priests of Babylonia, and those of Egypt, as the students of Tibetans monasteries, the Druids knew how much certain philosophical truths can become a poison for the unprepared minds, how much certain applications of science can be destructive. The secret was kept. The knowledge was oral. The ignorance was respected as long as one did not see in it the germ of transformation.

The Buddha did not write, Pythagoras and Jesus either. The pure truth ceases to be pure truth once it is mineralized in the stone of texts. It takes the winged character of speech to leave its true color and this color is changing, not by the act of the one who says the word, but the fact of the one who receives it. The mark of the highest wisdom is in this prudence that retains elements of knowledge and measures them to the reception capacity of the one who aspires to know. One must cry this lost extent, the revelation of knowledge, the pearl thrown to swine.

But by dint of silence, the oak children doctrine could have died with them. The fact of transmitting the truth is a great tragedy which unfolds since human origins. How to weigh what should be given, and when there is no one to receive, what to do with the divine gift?

The main data of the philosophy of the Druids have been retained in Ireland, where the Druids, chased of Gaul, fled to escape the "dark light" of the Roman civilization. They have been written down during the Middle Ages and exhumed in the last century[1]. In these texts, called the Book of Bardism, one must unravel the Christian influences

1 *Le Mystère des Bardes de l'île de Bretagne.* Translation by Adolphe Pictet, Geneva 1856.

and regain the old Druidic thought, abnormal thinking by its purity, strange by its eastern aspect, opposed to our customs, against our way of loving life, the eternal thought of the wise men.

* * *

Trees instead of statues! Vaults of trees instead of temples! Nothing but white robes for priests! Only boardwalk huts to shelter them! How the Christian clergy must have despised these wretched representatives of an incomprehensible cult whose liturgies were sung by winds, who once born, attired in mitres, gold crosses and dazzling uniforms.

The Druids knew the tragic role that gold played in the world and the intimate relationship that united it with the earthly evil. Violence is rarely exercised for the possession of a particular object, it is exercised for gold which is the representation of all that is desirable, because gold has a sort of supernatural power to condense desire. For centuries, Druids also banned in Gaul, the circulation of gold and proclaimed as a threatening reality, the curse attached to this metal.

When, after the Gallic invasions of Italy and Macedonia, Tolosates of the banks of the Garonne in Toulouse returned, the city of five suburbs, bringing back from east gold they had sacked, they could not keep their wealth. They were enjoined to rush it into a lake that was in the middle of the city. It is about the location of this lake that, according to the legend, a few centuries later was built the church of Saint-Sernin.

But came a time when the guardians of ancient forests could not resist the infiltration of gold. This happened long before the Roman invasion, perhaps with the return of the conquerors who left with Brennus. And it was the punishment for the distant accomplished looting.

The gold went up the Rhône with small boats. Its poisonous dust scattered along roads, penetrated the fortified towns that dominated it. The beautiful faces of Apollo engraved on the coins were reproduced by goldsmiths that seduced the handling of the royal metal. The curse was forgotten.

The greatest human fear is the fear of death. Yet, the Druids had com-

pletely liberated the Gauls from it. One can say that the fear of the afterlife, of its silence and its darkness is the characteristic of western races.
If the Druidic philosophy remained the insider sharing, their conception of death was popular and children, as soon as they were conscious
of living, were taught on the small value of life. The Gauls had realized Plato's view that the body is a prison and they were always ready
to leave this prison with joy. They offered themselves to death for the
slightest reason, not because their existence was devoid of happiness,
but because pleasures of superior quality awaited them after death, if
they had lived bravely and nobly.

Their belief in the future life was absolute, certain and ingenuous. They
frequently borrowed money for which repayment was to be performed
only in the other world and the smallest sense of trickery did not slip
into the borrower's soul. There were frequent communications with the
afterlife. The living wrote to the dead. All they had to do was to burn
their letter in a sacred fire so that they were assured that it reached more
accurately than by any postal service. Moreover they had the confirma-
tion by the answers of the dead, which were reported intuitively.

Suicides were common and they had to be regulated. The Druids
created boards of fixed man before which arose those who wanted to
commit suicide. The permission was only granted in virtue of valid reasons that were weighed and discussed carefully. If the permission was
denied, it was very rare that the candidate for suicide might override
as he feared further posthumous punishment.

The Druids had a concern that stretched to the future life. They placed
their ideal in human perfection and they were trying to move towards
this perfection, even the dark souls of thieves and criminals. Thus condemned to death suffered their sentences only after a period of five
years. Druids thought precisely that the bad man who is rushed into
the unconsciousness that follows death, with feelings of violence and
hatred, is not likely to improve and will return to the earth as bad as he
came out of it. So they made him undergo a training camp for death.

The basis of the philosophy of the Druids was the belief in the immortality of the soul and its endless transmigrations. Men who have

this faith, have totally different customs from those who do not have it. Their life has its place in a succession of other lives. It ceases to have an inestimable value as it will be replaced by another and so on ad infinitum. Death is only a passage and a transformation, losing its formidable character. It is a full of curiosity event that can, considered from a certain angle, be exciting and even infinitely desirable.

The Gauls from the Druids era, although this could not be questioned, as all historians of antiquity have confirmed it[1], believed in the transmigration of souls and in their rebirth in new bodies.

The theory of the transmigration of souls has a curious particularity. Exposed to certain intellects who do not know it, it is immediately adopted and considered proven. They carry it in them. But it causes to others a mysterious horror. They rather remove it, not to speak of it, even deny one could have believed in it. Thus Mr. Camille Jullian who grants to the testimony of Julius Caesar a blind faith, dares for the first time to express a doubt.

One clearly feels that he would have preferred that the Druids had another belief. Mr. Philéas Lebesgue who published a scholarly and interesting study of Druidism[2], seems to have the same revulsion. Many writers and philosophers in the presence of this doctrine, to which Pythagoras, Plato and Neo Platonists have signed up for, stand on a disgusted reserve. Can a philosophical idea become vulgar by the fact of its associations? Was this one compromised by the puerile uses that have made of it some spiritualists? But can one imagine Plato compromised? Or is it only held in suspicion because it is contrary to Christian Orthodoxy?

Julius Caesar, in the comments, had only noted in passing, casually, this unimportant belief, of barbarian peoples.

But all that was incomprehensible lights through it. We are accustomed to give to the life of our body, a sacred character and make cheap of the life of our soul on the fate of which we are uncertain. But isn't the op-

---

1 Strabo, Valerius Maximus, Julius Caesar, Diodorus of Sicily
2 "Le Druidisme" was published in the edition of March 1931 in the journal: *Atlantis*.

posite more logical? The wisdom of the Greco-Roman world said with the melancholic ghost of Achilles, that is was better to be a slave on earth than a king among the dead. The Gauls did not think that way. This explains many features of their customs that seemed senseless to the Romans. Thus, when a Gaul of any importance was dead and that his dead body was burning, there were members of his family or friends that went up on the same pyre as him. In this way, they were certain to pass together through the same transformations of the afterlife. Hindu spouses have practiced this use to the present day.

That explains the human sacrifices whose use was so reproached to Druids. These so-called sacrifices were not immolations in a cruel God but joyful departures of men eager to participate in the happier life that follows death.

Gauls funeral fashion was cremation because they knew the resolving power of the fire. The fire by destroying the body's physical atoms prevents the immaterial body to regain its disintegrating form. He raised the barrier of nothingness. The attachment for life could obscurely push the being into the darkness that follows death, to enter into the matter to which it can no longer access. The fire, by destroying and purifying, makes this error impossible. The more men have a taste for physical life the more they have in them a desire of material tombstones, parodying the houses of the living. The aspiration for the future life in more subtle terms, translates the funeral rite of the fire which only leaves what is incorruptible and eternal of the being. Furthermore, the fire is only needed for those who may fear the earthly calling, in virtue of their attachments. For those who in their lifetime have learned to detach, it matters little to be buried or to be burned. They cannot be tempted to return to their miserable corpse rotting.

Druids have never believed in a cruel God, similar to the Jehovah of the Jews or to the one who doomed the sinner to eternal hellfire. The fire only lasted for a minute, that of of the stake. The supreme deity was abstract, infinite, and unknowable, as the primary cause in the Brahmanical religion. It was useless to represent it by statues or to raise temples for it, because it was making it pass from the domain of essences to the one of materiality. God was the supreme spirit which the world, with its laws and its forms, was emanated.

The human destiny was fulfilled in three different worlds. Out of the immeasurable abyss, the being first passed by Annwn[1] the stay of unconsciousness where he transmigrated endlessly through the lower kingdoms. It was an anti-human period. Then he became man in the second world, Abred. There he was undergoing lengthy trials, he changed shape in pain and joy to the moment when, in virtue of its efforts, he reached an equilibrium point which represented the conquest of its freedom. He was then able to enter in the third world, Gwynfid, linked to the sun where he knew the plenitude of the being in the clear euphoria of the understanding. There he found the primitive genius, love and the memory of his long past.

The Greek philosopher Hecataeus, who lived more than three centuries before Christ and of whom remain only short fragments, reported a strange and ancient belief of priests from Great Britain. These priests were the Druids who taught that there were mountains in the moon and also deep abysses whose attractive force was exerted over the souls of earthly deaths. The dead coming out of their bodies were called in the region of the moon where they were staying before returning to earth. But not all of them. Those who were ready for Gwynfid, were driven back by the lunar influence and left once and for all to the sun.

The Druids probably heard symbolically the power of these lunar abysses. But we must remember that there is in the Hindu doctrines a world of the moon and a world of the sun where the dead are divided in virtue of a kind of spiritual density.

Druidism may be related to primitive Brahmanism. It is an eastern philosophy essentially and which represents an essential wisdom we have difficulty in understanding, and we are tempted to call madness.

"Not only the Druids proscribed writing,... but they also prohibited wine, squared stones constructions, the use of certain metals, including

1 I give only to memory these Welsh names, wishing to abstain as much as possible from this easy erudition of which so many authors demonstrate by providing unfamiliar words, easily copied, to give the illusion of a profound science.

perhaps iron. They banned images[1]..."

Behind these defenses, which will seem foolish to reasonable minds, we can rediscover the spirit that motivated them. Nothing lasting should be built by man on earth. The monuments, whether for worship of the gods or the welfare of manufacturers, are vanity buildings. Wanting to stop the course of its eternal transformation means offending the infinite spirit. Life is a rapid transition that one must not mark by any stop sign. The traveler who is living should not think of planting a tree or building a house. He also should not be distracted from the original idea in which is all beauty.

It is in the inner kingdom of the soul that monuments must be erected and that forests higher than those of Armoric, must project their branches. Gold and iron are not used for perfection. The man becomes great by staying simple, by becoming purer and more intelligent.

It is not a doctrine of despair, the one that teaches the same joy to die than to live.

1 Philéas Lebesgue

The disappearance of the Druids

There is no story about the disappearance of the Druids; no famous persecution. Men with white robes, forest dwellers, seem to have erased as the thought they were the representatives. By roads, through forests, on small boats, along the rivers, they moved north to reach Great Britain and Ireland, from where they came and which did not rang yet from the noise of axes against the wood of trees.

Julius Caesar had himself struck an oak tree in the forest near Marseille. Few centuries later, St. Martin made solemnly cut a pine tree not far from Autun, in a place dedicated to the ancient religion. These two gestures are symbolic of the double destruction of Druidism by Rome and Christianity.

But there is probably an age for the peoples as there is for the humans. A certain simplicity of customs, enthusiasm of nature, faith in a more perfect future life, are the work of youth. With maturity comes the love of pleasure in the development of passions.

Cities became of stone; on extended roads were organized relays and hostelries; commodities circulated from one end to the other of Gaul; businesses grew; the physical and immediate well-being drove back the promise of spiritual happiness in a world without form. And if it takes a long time to pass from a physical state to a state where the mind plays a greater role, only few years are enough to the mutual.

Gaul was the colony which adopted with great ease and joy, the customs of Rome. The more a soul is ingenious the more it is easily corrupted.

The Roman scum pounced ardently on this land where Caesar had put to death the greater part of energetic men.

Like the Atrebates, the last representative of the Gallic resistance against Caesar, after having fought for a long time as partisan in the forests of the north, decided to negotiate with the victors. He gave up the fight, provided he would not have to meet or even see a Roman from a distance, and this condition was granted to him. But its realization was impossible because there were Romans already everywhere. Wherever he went, Commius met one. He gathered his partisans and took the path of the sea to reach Great Britain. No doubt he had taken some revenge by leaving, as Caesar himself, irritated, went in his pursuit and tracked him to the ships that were supposed to take him.

Yet, when he and his men went on these ships, the tide was low, they were bogged down in the mud and the legionaries' eagles appeared on the horizon over the next hills.

It was Commius's faith that saved him. Still, he deployed the sailcloth, despite the obvious impossibility of sailing on the mud. The ships remained motionless. But afar Caesar saw the billowing sailcloth. Fooled by the distance, he thought he was too late and retraced his steps. The wind changed and the tide began to rise. The confident Commius, beyond the fact that he tricked Caesar, was able to cross the sea, found a kingdom in Great Britain and no longer saw Romans.

Many Druids followed him. Those who remained dug into the deepest parts of the forests where Mothers had already taken refuge. But the lives of these Gallic goddesses became more and more precarious. One will no longer brought them honey and milk. Thin female ghosts paled beside the sources, became more and more transparent to the point of not being perceived. The soul of the tree locked itself in the contraction of barks. Many hair that flown into the game of climbing plants, stopped wrapping in golden waterfalls. Between the teeth of polished pebbles, died the laughter of the fountains.

Druids communities became less numerous. Young people abandoned the sacred science and the arid studies. They stopped learning by heart the three hundred poems, stories of exploits and wonderful glorification of the race it was necessary to know to become a bard. They entered the Gallic cavalry, experienced the joy of wearing uniforms, taking part in the triumphal parades, traveling on the occasion of wars.

Pan, the great Pan is dead! cried a night on the Tyrrhenian Sea a very loud voice, output from who knows where, who was heard by the passengers and sailors of a ship that was captained by a certain a Tammuz.

The night voice whose extra human character was observed by all who heard it, first addressed directly to captain Tammuz and asked him: Tammuz, are you there? And when he replied shakily that he was there, the voice ordered him, when he would reach a shore, to announce to men that Pan, the great Pan, was dead. And there was in this injunction the mysterious authority that could only be attributed to a divine force.

The story made by Tammuz of this strange adventure, flew from mouth to mouth, and the Roman world was deeply struck by it. The emperor Tiberius ordered an investigation. Senators went to the islands neighboring the site, where had sounded the voice, they asked the witnesses and could not doubt the authenticity of the story. It did not explain why Tammuz, ordinary man of Egyptian origin, a sailor little inclined to mysticism, had been chosen for the announcement of this divine death. But there were men supposed to ensure that the gods sometimes lacked of discernment in choosing their messengers and that a certain ignorance of men could quite possibly be the mark of another world.

A deep reality corresponded to the mysterious message which resounded overnight. Pan is dead indeed, simultaneously as was born the Christian thought and with him the hope of an alliance of nature and the mind. It was in the same time that Tiberius banned religious worship of the Druids in Gaul. It was some time later that Suetonius, who commanded the legionaries of Britain, destroyed the Druidic brotherhood of the Mona Island, on the coast of Wales.

When his soldiers were about to land, they saw coming out of the woods, a long line of Druids, gathered in a circular way around their priestesses. The Druids had their hands raised to the sky. The priestesses were holding torches, and uttered incantations while shaking them, calling for help to the fire element. The community was probably trying to push back the enemy by the force of a magical ritual. But there is no magic that is not broken by unbelief. The ritual was not powerful enough and the Druids and priestesses were massacred. Tacitus, the historian, do not fail to add "the woods were destroyed devoted to their horrible superstitions."

The wisdom of primitive communities that can be found later in the instructions of the Rose Cross taught that it was necessary to comply with the religion of the country where one is staying. Christianity had extended his omnipotence on the west, brotherhoods of Druids turned to Christian monasteries. Ireland and Scotland, where the Druids had fled, were the countries of the first and largest abbeys. They embraced the ancient colleges of astronomers and philosophers.

In 1220, there was still a secret sanctuary in Kildare where burned a perpetual fire, maintained by virgins called the girls of fire. The archbishop of Dublin solemnly came to put it out as a remnant of past beliefs. Yet, with the death of this flame, coincided the end of the extermination of Albigensians in the south of France, by the crusade of Innocent III. History likes to mark here and there by symbols, the correspondence of the material world with the spiritual one.

The legacy of Albigensians

There is a close relation between the thought of Druids and the one of Albigensians. It is not in vain that the Swastika is engraved more frequently than in any other region of France, around Toulouse, along the Garonne and in the Pyreneans valleys. Its presence on the steles of roads indicated that the spirit had been there, and where he had been, he came back.

The messengers, who came from the east in the nineteenth century, brought the announcement of reconciliation of man with the divine and indicated the straight path of salvation, only served to revive a sleeping truth waiting to be awakened. Nicetas, the Bulgarian, when he came to organize the Albigensians churches, passed on his secrets to men who already possessed them in the depths of their hearts.

The land of Occitania was with Armorica, the chosen land of the Druids, the one where the mix of Celts with Aquitanians had produced a pure and altruistic race of men where the blue eyes of the color of dream, were combined to brown hair, the color of strength. Early Christianity had no trouble in conquering them and if St. Sernin was martyred in the name of the Roman gods, his radiant basilica arose after him in memory of his words of love and became the Palladium of Toulouse. But men of Occitania were also the first to suffer from the corruption of the Christian clergy, of its pomp and greed, to understand that there were only simulacrum left on altars and that the spirit of Christ lived elsewhere. The messengers had no trouble in showing them that it was in themselves that they had to find it.

There is only a small group of men that reaches the spiritual truths. If one is faithful to the doctrine of the Druids as the Albigensians, it must be thought that souls of those ones return together, at certain periods in new bodies, for purifying incarnations. They form throngs following each other and become less numerous as the best ones reach the goal, are stripped of desire, enter the Nirvana of the Hindus, in the Gwynfid of Druids, the ineffable sky of those who received the Cathar Consolamentum, in Plato's world of essences.

In reality, these throngs are expected to grow in number thanks to the natural power that the man who possesses a truth has of spreading it, through this virtue of bursting that one can assume to the truth. But it is not true. Throngs decrease from above and do not rise from below. The hatred of those who put enjoyment above all, work to destroy the doctrine of love wherever it appears and this destruction is made with a so perfect hypocrisy and a rigor so inexorable that it always triumphs.

The spirit of the Druids blew over the land of cut trees from north to south, through the voice of a few visionaries who could not help of preaching the message coming from the east, they checked in the internal book. That was the great tragedy of the war of Albigensians. It ended in the fall of the Château de Montségur where had fled the Saints and the perfects of Catharism.

There was a spiritual transmission of Druids to Albigensians. Men of the twelfth century, while walking on the roads of Lauragais or those of the county of Foix, regained an invisible legacy. The voice of the wise and simple fathers came out of the ground and spoke to them. It was the eternal inheritance that the Druids themselves had received from older fathers.

It is difficult to measure the links of a chain as secret, to establish with texts a parentage of elements so distant and so diverse. For thousands of year the poems of Vedas in India were transmitted orally. Druids proscribed writing. If the Albigensians have had books, they were burned in the wars and then in the trials of the Inquisition. It is only by shadows of evidence that one can physically join men separated by distances and centuries.

But the evidence of a relationship of speech that starts in Himalayas and spreads across the world through messengers yet exists, and if added together, they give a certainty.

There are the Orphic poems verses that seem translated word for word from the hymns of the Vedas[1]. A biography of the Buddha circulated in the west in the eleventh and twelfth century and the Christianized version of this biography is the novel of Barlaam and Josaphat[2]. The recantation spell required to the Byzantium of the Cathars was found and there is the Buddha's name alongside that of Manes[3].

Always the same wisdom circulated among men telling them same things. The soul is immortal and must pass through many lifetimes to regain the divine state. As stated in the interviews of the Buddha, as it is said in the Gospel, one must lead a simple life, despise riches, give up pleasure, and strive towards the spirit.

Those who have gathered to free themselves by mutual momentum and educate those who do not know differed on many points. But if, by breaking the laws of time, it was possible to reunite the monks of Tibet, the Therapeutae from the lake Maria near Alexandria, the Essenes of Mar Saba near the Dead Sea, the Pythagoreans of Sybaris, the Druids of Gaul and the Albigensians of Montségur, certainly, despite the difference of languages, they would easily understand each other. And maybe that the members of this assembly impossible to perform, would be dressed in the same way, with the same white linen robe, the emblem of purity. All during the meal would ask the same food. They would join hands in the same way and would look into themselves to pray. At the time when the sun is not up yet but will soon appear, they would accomplish the same ritual.

All have practiced this ritual, and this universality is the sign that is must have a unique value. The fulfillment of a symbolic act has repercussions in the spiritual life. Men dressed in white, regardless of time and place, just before daybreak, were standing, face turned towards the east and had greeted the morning light as the arrival of a spirit. And the spirit came upon them, by the power of invocation, to the extent

1 According to Emile Burnouf.
2 According to Salomon Reinach who, certainly, cannot be accused of a too vivid imagination! (*Mythes et Religions*, Volume V).
3 This should convince those who cannot bear the idea that the Buddhist thought is found in Catharism.

where it had to be received.

Are there still men, nowadays, who, standing before dawn, call upon the rising spirit? And if there are, where are they?

The last coming of messengers

How to explain the contempt and oblivion into which the Druids were held by their descendants? How to explain the careless tone of great historians such as Michelet and Camille Jullian towards them. We can hardly we quote some writers as Jean Reynaud, Alexandre Bertrand, Philéas Lebesgue, who understood and loved Druidism. It is the same for the philosophy of the Druids as for the one of India. Curious minds study and explain it with abundance but there is between the pages of their books a hidden hostility and sometimes hatred.

The same contempt and ignorance have stricken the Albigensians. But for them, we can see the mechanism by which their memory had been covered up.

The church used for Catharism the method by which it was always successful with heresy it considered impressive. It has firstly attributed to the Cathars strange and horrible crimes and it has distorted their doctrine.

Druids have come down through centuries with the accusation of human sacrifices related to their name. (Michelet goes so far that he indicates that they "pierced the victim above the diaphragm" and he lists specific details that one would be tempted to believe, without the improbability of the matter, that one was an eyewitness of the scene I). But the church has not exercised its resentment on Druids. If they are secretly hated it is because of the relatedness of their doctrine, a relatedness which can be found among the Albigensians, with early Christianity.

Peoples who call themselves Christians have a fundamental horror of the thought of the true Christianity. Christianity of the early Christians is eminently antisocial and the application of its principles would lead to a rapid separation of the family, the property, the society. Its essence, as the one of the Druidism and the one of Buddhism is a negation of the physical life since it places all ideal in the life of the afterlife.

To detach from what one possesses! To be less selfish! To enjoy less passionately in its flesh! Men will never want to consent to what appears on their staked reason as a decrease of themselves. The great missionaries come through the ages, they teach the doctrine of renunciation and they pass. They are given in a corner of the soul a theoretical reverence and we try to forget them.

But maybe that the great missionaries will cease to present themselves. A favorable ground is needed for the forming of a movement as the one of Albigensians, resulting from the Druidic thought. It is possible that the mechanical form taken by the actual life is forever contrary to this outbreak. There is a madness of the regress called the forward march, the progress. The Gaul of the Gauls, despite the unparalleled extermination of Julius Caesar, welcomed with euphoria, merchants and collectors of Roman taxes because they introduced more favorable conditions for physical life. The more we move forward in history the more we see declining the importance of spiritual factors. In the fourth century, one was fighting in Alexandria and in Corinth for theological points. That time has passed. Nothing similar can be imagined today. The more one goes, the more the mind loses its importance. The elites will soon only care about economics.

Then, there is an end to the earthly race of the pure and good. They came, they offered the light they had because they had called and sought with love, but will they come back?

In our country, these pure and good were Druids and Albigensians. Druids for centuries that one has not determined the number, have made our ancestors untroubled, free and happy men. Long after, Albigensians appeared in only one province, the one where the land had kept the old ideal of dead trees, the detachment[1], and one made them all perish. Now, we do not see any sign of a revival of the lost doctrine. It seems that the generation that brings more souls outputs from who knows where, which are embodied in the skulls where throbs only primitive

---

1 The word can be taken both ways, material and spiritual. The detachment is proper to the ideal of the tree.

appetite to enjoy with her bones, nerves and flesh. It may be that the admirable passerbies never pass again.

From here and there, few solitary[1] individuals attempt to evoke obscurely the wisdom of their fathers. But it is a necromancy which only calls useless ghosts.

In fact, these last defenders of the perennial philosophy, lacking of "these archival documents", of "this authentic texts" of which gargle modern scholars, will be charged of creating legends and will be called imposters. Illuminated by artificial footlights, the Druid will shed forever its mistletoe in the veil of a Veleda of theater. The Albigensian, more unknown, will fade more and more on its mysterious mountain of Allège.

Perhaps it has a good thing. An astonishing ardor, such a patient continuity to reject this higher form of truth is probably a sign that it is not made for men to whom it was offered. It is a powerful and truthful speech, the one that says: "No one should be forcibly dragged to heaven."

1 There is in Brittany a college of Bards of Armorica which gathered the debris of the tradition and tries to perpetuate it. The illustrated journals have recently published photographs of their ceremonies. I jumped eagerly on them when they appeared. But horror! They reproduced more or less the old outdated images. This is not a reason, however, for the old Druidic spirit not to resurrect in this college.

MERLIN THE MAGICIAN

The son of the incubus

The souls of all forests were not dead yet in the fifth century. Some were still alive enough to be born of them, literally, as we shall see, a genius Druid whose activity animated the entire Western literature during the ten centuries that followed.

Naturally, many historians, many but not all, have denied Merlin's existence. Not because of his paternity directly green, because we can at a pinch find a human explanation to his birth, but because of a natural love of denial.

The enchanting epithet attached itself to Merlin's name and it is a reason, according to history, to place his existence in doubt. Any character who practices somewhat magic, even if he is very tall, destroy thereby its historical reality. As in Antiquity, Appolonius of Tyana and Simon the Sorcerer. In modern times, the opinion that the Count of St. Germain and Cagliostro have never existed and are only heroes of Alexandre Dumas, would be greeted with a mysterious satisfaction and quickly adopted. The same shall apply in a century, for the monk Rasputin.

Furthermore, the existence of all those who play a spiritual role and have the greatest human influence is denied by a certain class of unbelievers who are irritated by the mere fact of existence, yet normal. Thus, Buddha, Jesus Christ, Pythagoras, Zoroaster, Homer, Shakespeare and recently Socrates[1], have been accused of not having real existence. This basically would not matter if in the essence of this denial was not hiding a taste of diminishing ideas, to remove them of their prestige by making them collective. But if we examine these denials, we can notice that the assumptions made to defend them are much more unlikely than the hypothesis of the character's existence, according to the legend, even if it is adorned by a certain number of miracles. It is often the enemy of the splendid, the scholar with archival materials who requires the

1 E. Dupréel: *La légende Socratique*. Brussels, 1922.

greatest amount of credulity.

This is how Merlin was born, according to the legendary truth translated by the bishop and historian Gildas, who was his contemporary.
Despite his book that remained: *De Excidio Britannicae*, despite several
biographies written by monks and one possesses, the existence of the
historian himself has been put in doubt. However, as there are three,
also saints, who have at the same period left letters and books, it is likely
that one, at least, really existed.

First and foremost, it should be known that in the fifth century in
Great Britain, "there was in a canton of the Silures country, an incubus
spirit which was in love with a young girl."

It is widely known what an incubated spirit is. It is a male creature,
but of extra human essence. It is our thoughts that by materializing
themselves create incubi, although in some cases, the situation could
change and they can have another origin. Thus they are of a more vivid
race. The incubi have a gift of physical possession which is hard to believe as long as one did not felt it. This gift is proportional to the quality and accuracy of lustful images by which the incubus has been fed.
Moreover, it is not always sexual and according to the soul which calls
it and gives it substance, it can have a perfect dream character. But it is
rare, the generating vitality being the essential element which allows it
to get to the form, or its illusion, which is the same thing.

The incubi and succubi first raise the question of the reality of their
existence. Unfortunately, those who are visited by these creatures tell
little of it and it is quite universally admitted among the cultivated
minds that without further examination, one should consider it as superstition and folly.

The facilities that modern society gives to the leanings of physical
love to achieve, decreased to enormous proportions incubi and succubi.
However many confidences of single-handed conclude the nocturnal
presence of a being that would "almost" have the attributes of reality.

All the cases of young girls being pregnant, swearing that they do
not understand its reason and that there is no physical cause for a next
birth, should be clarified. Assuming that most of them lie for any fam-

ily reason or to deceive an unsuspecting fiancé, there must be a limited number, infinitely small, that do not lie and have been visited by an incubus. For the most certain physical evidence of the reality of the incubus is this generating capacity.

According to Saint Augustine "the amount and seriousness of testimonials which attest the reality of incubi and succubi, make the denial almost impossible."

The Middle Ages has in the records of its procedures a large number of undeniable cases of young girls they said possessed, and accurately watched because of this, have given birth to incubi children. The fact of having a father composed only of coagulated fluidic substance would result, in a child of a small size, with bleary eyes, very short-sighted and of stupid wickedness.

Depending on the country, they were called Selkind, Cambion or Kikrops. These creatures lived shortly and were progressing. They had acquired from birth all the development of which they were capable. There are no traces of them in countries of the south, while Germany reported a large number. But that number has decreased over the centuries.

There must have been beautiful and intelligent Selkinds and Cambions. But the church having assimilated them to demons, preferred to report only their ugliness and their evil of power, in compliance with the popular idea of the devil. But those were perhaps from another category of beings that included the incubated spirit reported by the bishop Gildas.

This incubated spirit that inhabited the southern coast of Cambria, haunted preferably a valley called the Basalik Valley. He was a genius of these forests that stood still, immutable and tall, around the land cultivated by men. He was known and even famous since another ecclesiastical writer of the era claims to have been in contact with him and have benefited from his prophetic qualities. Geniuses, commonly called Duz, were sometimes of aerial order, at times of plant order but still of a luxurious kind. This one saw one day a young girl and he fell in love with her.

This young girl was a priestess of a local and Druidic cult. These cults persisted in Britain, they sided with Christianity and mingled with it.

The young girl of the Basalik Valley, knew as her kind, the dangers that lied in the forests for the daughters of men. But she was priestess and felt perhaps physically attracted to the geniuses she invoked. Maybe she chose in good conscience, to unit to a Duz than to a man. She fell asleep on a summer day, in the shade of trees and the Duz called by the dream of the young girl came to her and possessed her in her sleep.

The priestesses who violated their vow of chastity were sentenced to death. But it was not the same course if the wish had been violated with a genius of trees, which, according to the authors of the time, happened quite frequently.

Bishop Gildas, whose story has been taken into account, was obliged to respect the venerable character of this paternity. The people clung to Christianity but he respected the geniuses of its forests. The child directly born of the venerable trees had a sacred character. More was expected of him as from an ordinary man's son. The popular judgment was not mistaken with the child that was Merlin.

The master of snakes

The child conceived by the women who had fallen asleep in the forest, received the name of Ambroise and the surname Merlin, given to him because of the companions of his childhood. Merlin is the Frenchified name of Marzin in Armorican, Myrdhin in Welsh and Meller in Scots, and it means: the one who lives with snakes.

There is a mystery in the relationships of snakes and men that has never been fully elucidated. In all countries, some individuals enjoy a mysterious authority on snakes. They call them and they come, they handle them without provoking their anger and in some cases, they take from them warnings and forecasts related to future events.

These individuals have existed in all times because we see them mentioned by travellers of all ages. They were called Marsi in Italy and in Gaul, Psylli in Africa, and Ophiogenes in the islands of Greece. They still exist nowadays almost everywhere, but is seems that they are the most numerous in Egypt and Ethiopia. What is curious is that their power to charm snakes is hereditary. Even when they are ignorant charlatans, which is often the case, they claim a strange alliance which would have existed between their ancestors and the people of snakes.

Nowadays, a traveller who stays in any hotel of Cairo is very lucky, by speaking with a doorman, to be linked to a miserable looking man who accomplishes a quite surprising phenomenon. He visits the place that is designated to him, a garden or a cultivated field even very distant and whatever this place, having recited in a low voice and as for himself, a mantra in an unknown language maybe to him, he will make snakes come out of the ground. This snakes are sometimes numerous and come winding docilely around his arms. If one asks this man for the explanation of his power, he speaks of his filiation with King Solomon, whose domination extended over snakes.

This is not the place to deal with this fascinating subject. But it may be noted that if, nowadays, being charmer of snakes is a condemned profession or if the relationships with animals of this species are left to guardians of menageries and to a small number of naturalists, it was otherwise in other times, more enlightened than ours, in a number of views. The most eminent sages applied to the attendance of snakes and they found in this spiritual profit that we find hard to imagine. We know nothing of the methods that were theirs. Moreover, the very idea that there might be methods to communicate with snakes could only provoke the cheerfulness of rational men who call themselves scientists. And I suppose that some naturalists who have specialized in the study of snakes are unanimously ready to declare that only is interesting with them the knowledge of their venoms and their use in medicine.

Yet there was in Antiquity, men who drew from their relations with snakes, benefits in the order of perspicacity and divination. Maybe they assumed that if one speaks to an animal for a result which is not material, it is not to itself that one should speak, but to the collective soul of its kind. They must have known that the then language is not made by sounds or signs. The communication was to establish by states of ecstasy. The legendary pact of alliance with animals, which tradition remains confused in the mind of the Bohemian one meets along the way, the Egyptian fortune teller, must have had all its power. Among all species, the snake has a virtue relative to the power of intelligence. It is not in vain that the Hebrew legend makes the snake of the antic story of the tree of good and evil, play a significant role. The collective soul of snakes is a powerful entity more subtle than that of other animal species, more eager of spiritual food that the divine order will only allow to taste in subsequent cycles. If each soul of species has already adopted a way of transformation of its own, it is the taste of intelligence which dominates in the soul of the snake and the venom is maybe the only physical form of its powerless rage to convey so slowly towards the mind, to park for myriads of years in the crawling animality.

But this soul, despite the limits imposed by the inevitable cyclical laws, is full of wisdom, responsible for knowledge. Not the soul of a snake of course, limited to its food, its eggs, to the sun-ray which warms it, but the collective soul of all, from the fragile, which only think of biting with poisonous teeth, to the huge, which ardently desire the friendship of men.

There were, in past centuries, men better informed than we are of invisible forces, more in line with the soul of the world and the various souls of which it is formed, who obtained animal wisdoms, some secrets which man could not individually reach.

Part of these ancient magicians was undoubtedly this King Psyllus of whom Pliny speaks, whose tomb still existed in his time. This Psyllus, who gave his name to Psylli, is behind the legend of the pact. It was him who founded the school of magic whose teaching spread in the West. Maybe he communicated with the Druids and taught them a method that can be found nowadays in all snake charmers. They first enter in a state of trance and use either perfumes or music to share this trance to snakes on which they act. The travelers Bruce and Forskhal, speaking of charmers of Abyssinia where the tradition of Psyllus must remain, say that it is by taking a bath in the juice of certain herbs that they gain their power over snakes. But here it is only a question of material power. The psychological communication, the meeting of the collective soul on a different level than the human one, was obtained through perfumes. And this is part of the lost secrets, even more lost than the mere mention of their existence calls into question the good faith of whoever sets it.

In the days of Merlin, the title of man of snakes was not a second-rate title. Forests of Great Britain had resisted to the human ax and even extended to the thresholds of seas. Snakes were its numerous and impressive inhabitants, and the one who had made an alliance with them took part of their power.

Maybe it was due to the powers of divination Merlin held from them that he had a great reputation since his youth. Unfortunately, the ecclesiastical writings that speak of him only allow to know the great lines of his life. Student of the Druids, and Druid himself, Merlin received in colleges of these wise men, the science they owned. He learned the twenty thousand lines where was locked the history and the philosophy of the past, from the mouth of Taliesin, of Llywarch Hen, of Aneirin, the Druids whose names remain through the curses of the bishop Gildas.

Great Britain then fought against the Saxons invasions. Vortigern, military leader of the tribes, called to him as an adviser. When this chief died, he remained with his successor, who is known as King Arthur.

It is then that a lamp relights, the ancient flame of lost initiations, flame continuously extinguished, always re-emerging. The spirit of wisdom is not dead, it shall be eternally carried across the earth, so great the barbarism and ignorance, by disinterested messengers. It is the darkest time in human history. Everywhere, from the north, blond men with braided hair, arrived in countless troops, plundering cities, destroying temples, taking it out on statues, especially on what is a spiritual symbol or an image of beauty. In Athens the schools of philosophy have been closed and the last masters of thought have been forced into exile in Persia. The Library of Alexandria was burned. Christianity has seen its first wave got tangled up in human hardness and is mineralized in dogmas and hierarchies.

Yet, the spirit must be saved, there has to be strong men to defend it, holy men to reveal it. The Druids will change of appearance. They will transmit the message under a new form and this form will come under the sign of Jesus.

It is Merlin the Druid who gives the first watchword by establishing the Knights of the Round Table, the world has changed. The ideal now rests in the mystical Grail vase. But whatever the external shape of its symbol, no matter whether it is Christ's true blood or the illumination of the mind. The bottom line is that there are men to believe in it[1].

---

1 The union of snakes and of the first wise men is attested by many legends. In India, the Nagpurians of the city of Nagpur, which were primitive ascetics, are represented with human heads and snake tails. The ancient Chinese encyclopedia gives the portraits of these early initiators. They are also half human, half snake.

The mysterious islands

We find repeatedly, in the legendary lives of Merlin, allusions to mysterious islands, islands where one is seeking salvation, inhabited by wise and pure men or magician priestesses. It is sometimes the Île de Sena or the Île de Sein, at times the Avalon Island, sometimes other islands which are not named and are placed somewhere on the side of the West, among the fogs of the unknown seas.

When Merlin has to hand over to King Arthur a magical sword which will give him victory, he embarks to the Avalon Island. It is only there, in the school of Druids who live secluded in the solitude of the island, that the rites can be made, of which the sword will draw its power. This is obviously the episode of a chivalric romance but can hide some truth.

The islands, by the protection that offered their situation, always were the shelters of wise men, eager to indulge in art and science, far from the savagery of men. It is in the islands that travelers meet characters gifted with powers which seem supernatural to them. It is there also that hides the Druidic science to its decline.

In the Odyssey, Odysseus, after a long journey arrived in a country where the nights are shorter. He reached the Île d'Yeu, which is inhabited by the sorceress Circe and other magicians. Everyone agreed, in Roman times, to place the Île d'Yeu in the extreme western point of Gaul. This point is the Île de Sein.

It is in this region that was located the mysterious island of the Blessed, where went after death souls of those who had led a pious life. There, among the silver poplars and the cloudy myrtles, ancient dead tasted a little sad happiness, the more sad because it had to be eternal.

On Circe's indications, Odysseus reached a magical shore, a one day sailing from the island of Sein, where the dead rushed when he has shed blood of which the vapor feeds them, and has made the necessary rites so he could see and hear them. It is also on a hyperborean island that the hero Homer talks to his former dead companions and gather all the deeply melancholic impressions that life in the afterlife leaves them. Such is the difference of souls, according races where they came to incarnate. Life after death is a miserable condition for Greeks. It appears to Gauls of the same period as a sporty and cheerful appearance.

On the other hand, the historian Mela, puts in the Île de Sein, nine priestesses which specialized in divination and were used to say the future to sailors who stopped in their island. Strabo speaks if an island exclusively inhabited by women, located at the mouth of the Loire. This island was the Île de Batz where women were Druidesses.

Thus, islands surrounding Gaul housed secret colleges where went the most educated Druids and where lived young girls devoted to virginity in order to develop these gifts of clairvoyance, which are always inseparable from a chaste life. This is what gave to these islands this halo of mystery and made that in legends and novels of Middle Ages, the knight who needed for his weapons, a magical consecration, sailed with a guide with a long robe and a long beard, symbols of wisdom, to reach across the waves a mystical citadel of truth.

If all the mysterious islands are located to the West, after this granite high wall of which became the Armorican land in front of the ocean, even so there were still colleges of Druids in the islands of the Mediterranean. One of them occupied the Lérins Islands, in front of Cannes, long before the arrival of Saint Honoratus. This college was next to a temple erected in honor of a fabulous hero, Lero, whose shadows of times veil history forever. These Druids left with the first Roman invasions. Pliny says that in his lifetime, were kept under the city name of virgins, the memories of a group of women who would have inhabited the Île de Lero but of which remained no trace.

It should be noted that when Honoratus came to found an abbey on one of the two islands of Lérins, which since kept the name Lérins, he found a prodigious number of snakes he hastened to destroy. These snakes, like the ones in Psylli, like the ones of the priestesses of Dionysus in Thrace, as those who gave their name to Merlin, were once sacred snakes and became savage by the abandonment of the priests who had made an alliance with them.

Well-considered wise men, instead of monks blinded by their hatred of paganism, had attempted to renew the ancient pact.

No one thought of it.

Brocéliande and the Lady of the Lake

It is in the very distant past that one must look for the origin of a certain form of stupidity which is commonly referred to as the French spirit, this French spirit which, when it tilts toward rudeness, receives the name of Gallic spirit.

The story of Merlin is a curious example of the distortion of the true wisdom of our fathers in favor of a way of thinking that the skepticism of the Roman society brought, which developed with Christianity and stifled over the centuries this joyful purity based on the brotherhood with nature that was characteristic of the Gauls before Caesar.

When the novels of chivalry began to interpret the story of Merlin, the understanding was already lost. The effort of all authors of poems, Robert de Boron, Chrétien de Troyes, Wolfram von Eschenbach and of all anonymous writers, tried to Christianize the Druid and transform the meaning of his legend. One imposed him a conception of feminine love as conceived by the novels of chivalry and which could not be his. One made of this wise philosopher an old man possessed by senile desires.

One transformed the Lady of the Lake, symbol of intelligence, in a maddening courtesan character. Moreover this female puppet must be a form almost eternal of popular desires just as the lower literature which flatters them. Even today, it remains the basis of plays and famous films and our great psychologists make tirelessly new creations always found original. Finally, one imagined that Merlin, converted to Christianity by holy characters, had denied his philosophical errors and had returned to the church.

This was the bad fate of the Druids as Merlin's, for only having historians with no real love for the essence of their thought and unable to revive a way of being strange and unconceivable for us, but it is necessary nevertheless to try to find if one want to understand them. I will quote only one example, about Mr. de la Villemarqué, Merlin's historian of the nineteenth century whose opinion is an authority on the subject. It is about the ecstatic elation state in which put themselves Druidic bards, to obtain phenomenon of divination and enter in communication, on a different level, with creatures of a different kind than the human one. In a general way these elations to reach ecstasy were practiced in most cults of Antiquity. The output of the body was an elementary exercise. There was no candidate for religious initiation who that had not known the processes of externalization to achieve a more subtle level. All that is known of the Druidic science suggests that the Druids found in these states means of communication with plant and animal souls. It seems that nowadays in Brittany, in virtue of an obstinate survival, some states of enthusiasm are still called evil of Merlin.

Medieval poems speak of Merlin's madness. This madness must have only been his ability to enter a state of lyrical and divinatory trance. But what about the serious and contained indignation tone of Mr. de la Villemarqué, speaking of an inspired bard, in a similar state of trance. "Is it necessary to add that this madman was driven from vision to dangerous folly and from folly to death." And when questioned about what should have been thought of these states, Mr. de la Villemarqué is hiding behind the opinion of François de Salles. "No wonder if the malicious spirit, to play the monkey, mislead the souls, scandalize weak ones, operates raptures to few souls less solidly educated in true devotion."

The true story of Merlin's life is little known. He fought with King Arthur against the Saxons invaders of Great Britain. But perhaps the detail of his actions would be of no education. It is his prophesies and his disappearance that have earned him an enormous influence for ten centuries. His prophesies which circulated orally, were published in the twelfth century. As the ones that was supposed to make later Nostradamus, they have an enigmatic character. Each prophet slightly shrewd gives to his prophesies the ambiguous character that fate itself has. The ambiguity of Merlin's prophesies allowed them for a long time to be true. One can be aware now that his essential prophesy did not realized itself. He had announced the defeat of the Saxons and foreign races which/who oppressed Great Britain and the victory of the first inhabitants of Armorica. It never happened. But during the centuries more than one political event was recognized being announced by Merlin. And even if there were no exact true coincidence between the predictions and the events, these predictions favorable to the Breton race, were animated by the popular faith and gave a comforting aliment of hope which perpetuated for centuries. It is the authentic role of predictions.

Merlin had the wisdom no to die but to disappear. Just as other wise men when their time had come. Empedocles went for a walk on the edge of Mount Etna and did not come back. Apollonius of Tyana entered in a temple, in Diktynna to meditate and disappeared. The Hindu philosopher Sankaracharya never came out of a cave where he had entered. After the battle of Arderidd where it is believed that King Arthur died, from this point forward Merlin decided that he preferred to live with the animals of the forest which seemed to him less savage than men, and he went deep into the Brocéliande forest of which he probably did not come out.

The Brocéliande forest is located between Rennes and Brest, close to the small city of Montfort and is called today Paimpont forest. Carved, fragmented, crossed by paths, it is now a small forest producing logging. But in the fifth century it was a place of inaccessible depths, whose secrets had to be known to enter.

There must have been a refugee group of the last Druids of Gaul, a hidden community to which Merlin probably belonged. He only came back among his own to complete his life far from the world's barbarism that was growing.

How long the Druids of the Brocéliande forest carried on, next to this fountain of Barenton whose water had the property of giving eternal youth? No one can know.

The neighborhood residents who created the legend knew only that in the heart of the deep forest where only few loggers ventured, lived men immersed in inaccessible studies, in mysterious contemplations. They only retained that the purpose of the inexplicable activity of these men was intelligence, this principle to which they had only a vague connection, which even seemed terrible to them, but to which they attributed qualities of light and beauty. Under the centenarian's trees, they still represented young men by the activity of the research, which developed the mysterious intelligence. The principle of light became at length for them, more and more confusing. They showed, by the dark spireas, a vague light floating above the forest, silvering the tops of giant oaks. This clarity personified by a fairy who was the Lady of the Lake.

Merlin never came out of the Brocéliande forest again. No one ever saw him again. The intelligence, with the powerful attractions of study, the limitless paradises of the mystical contemplation, held him prisoner. Henceforth he inhabited the magical palace of the mind, a palace whose poet's imaginations cannot paint the beauty. Authors of novels of chivalry will try, with recollections of palaces glimpsed in Antioch and in Jerusalem during the Crusades, to unfold the marble stairs, painted colonnades of porphyry, along paved mosaic galleries. They will only materialize an ideal splendor which does not look like their roman invasions. They will make the princesses with braided hair walk on the mosaics. But the entire dream they will give to their attitudes cannot disguise the physical attraction of their bodies. Heroes covered with armors, have crossed the earth to bring a talisman and returned, because of some divine mission. No one will be fooled by their word. Everyone will know that they are the indicators of the reign of the force, that they pursue the possession of temporal goods, with a divine pretext.

Authors of novels will transform the light floating above the forest, the pure light which became the Lady of the Lake, into a woman of flesh that will embody the material pleasure of the senses. After a few centuries, the symbol of air ceases to be included. If Merlin decided to withdraw in the forest, if he desired to complete his life away from men, it can only be because he wanted to devote himself to the female pleasure, only because he met the Lady of the Lake, the woman of pleasure. And in this form, the Lady of the Lake became the ideal secret of each. The true Gallic spirit is dead. The pact with nature is therefore silent and incomprehensible. No one can explain that the wise withdraw to study and meditate. If he withdraws from the world, the only reason must be to enjoy materially near a seductive woman whose charms are only those of pleasure.

When Merlin disappears, darkness from the interior of souls, have recovered not only Gaul, but Europe. Early Christianity vanished and those who carry the flame in their heart took refuge in convents. It is in the convents that the spiritual strength of the world is hiding and is immobilized. Churched are erected in cities with their gold ornaments, gold hunting of their relics, golden uniforms of their bishops. The reign of the force begins. This is the time of bad kings and bad emperors. Soon, there will only be art parodies and caricatures of philosophy. Charlemagne will appear. Gothic and Germans barbarians gathered around him, will form an academy, germ of future academies, where Charlemagne will be called King David and whose members will take the names of Homer, Plato and of great men of Antiquity, in order to cover their ignorance under false names.

The Druidic spirit is clearly dead. Merlin went back to find the last Druids in this Brocéliande forest which later, will be stripped even of its name. This start is a broader symbol of what happens in certain periods of history. There are times when peoples are abandoned by the spiritual element which guides them. The conditions of existence become some-times so oppressive, so physical, that a certain class of men cannot live there. They then disappear to go to other countries and they embody no more in races from where the spirit is banned.

This is what happened to Druids. Merlin is the last to be known. But before disappearing, he laid the foundations of a secret group that would allow, among the darkness of centuries that were coming, to truth to be transmitted and intelligence to be perpetuated. When ignorance triumphs and that force dominates, it is necessary that the lamp of the mind is not extinguished and that its messengers are able to pass it from hand to hand.

Of this secret order founded by Merlin one only knew the name: the order of the Knights of the Round Table. Perhaps it was not called like this and had no name. The material detail of a table with a round form in a purpose of equality for those who would sit there, was what struck the minds, despite its little importance. One has retained the form of the table around which men gathered without wondering why exactly they met. It is by this order, of which was made with no reason, an order of warriors, because it is not by the strikes of a sword that one conquers the truth, that the Druidic tradition, the pure tradition of the Gallic land was to be perpetuated. This tradition which contained the secret of salvation, the path that leads man to the divine state, received the symbolic name Grail.

Merlin could sleep in the Brocéliande forest. He had accomplished the task incumbent on the last Druid. The essential secret contained in the Grail would be transmitted to those who would be worthy. The order of the Round Table was charged of this transmission that ignorant men should not have known. So few that are the intelligent ones lost in the barbaric times, they would find in their time, the education entitled to those who sincerely aspire to the divine light.

Merlin, according to the primitive legend, had struggled to win the Lady of the Lake. It did not matter if he was alive or dead. Because once one has reached the intelligence, one keeps it, whether being dead or alive.

One even possesses it more completely when being dead.

THE LEGEND OF THE GRAIL

The secret of Jesus

There is a liberating secret that has been transmitted since the beginning of the world.

The first men who were thrown on earth, either in virtue of a divine play, either as a result of some original sin, had received, with the key to an invisible door, the way out of the terrestrial world. This key which was made of any metal had to remain secret. His possession, prerogative of a small number was the principle of essential mysteries, the subject of a sacred transmission. There was something, mystical talisman, prays for deep resonances, animated words of power, that was only understandable for some wise men and which had to be transmitted by them to other chosen ones.

Why the secret was not to be revealed? Was it because it would not be understood? But the ban was then useless, and fell of itself. Was it under the desire of the one privileged by knowledge to keep their privilege? But one will see that the nature of privilege was such, that it was lost as soon as it was received. Was it not rather because the secret had maybe something contrary to the divine order and violated a fundamental law of nature?

The secret has strolled through the ages. All great teachers knew it and revealed it to their followers. Even the greatest teachers, like Buddha and after him Jesus, did not hesitate to make it public. They violated then the principle that governed the mysteries in all ages.

Buddha and Jesus had to be considered by other teachers without fame as imprudent whistle-blowers forgetful of the ancient oath. Those teachers had feared that this kind of betrayal was the source of great evils for humanity. But if they believed in the human incomprehension they never imagined it would reach this surprising degree. The secret was revealed and Ton realized that it would hardly change anything, over the world. An order of sublime truth can be displayed at all intersections, without modifying the blinkered beatitude of passersby.

I teach a doctrine of liberation, said Buddha. My kingdom is not from this world, said Jesus.

Yet men, by no means, did they thought of being freed and they clung with more roughness than ever to the kingdom of the earth. The secret having been revealed became once more, by itself, a secret.

The revelation had only been partial. A great revelation always has several degrees.

"Then Jesus Christ taught to Joseph of Arimathea the secret words that no one can narrate, or write, unless he has read the great book where they are recorded and these are the words that Ton pronounce at the moment of the consecration of the Grail, that is to say of the chalice."

These words are found in the novel of the Holy Grail of Robert de Boron, trouvère of Lorraine, who accompanied Richard de Montbéliard to the crusade and on the Cyprus Island. This writer had the taste of good deeds, chivalrous and pious deeds and he wanted to charm men of his time with stories, without rear mystical thought. He inspired himself by the rest of the legends which ran through West. But speaking of the Holy Grail, of the vase which contained the blood of Christ, it brought a tradition that was circulating on the lips of poets and that was transmitted, without granting it a great importance.

During a meal at Simon's that had taken place not long before his death, Jesus had used a vase, a chalice, the Grail and he had accomplished a ritual, made a ceremony. Speaking to Joseph of Arimathea, the possessor of the Grail, he had "taught him secret words that no one can narrate or write". He had spoken of a consecration, he had taught him a secret.

This secret was the essence of the teaching he had given, which could not be told to everyone but could not be lost. Joseph of Arimathea had carried it with him across the world, to the furthest limits of the West. But what had he done with it? To who had he bequeathed it?

Through the dark centuries of the Middle Ages, during the period when church, now immobilized in its gangue of gold and stone, spreads on the world its organization, there is a winged idea which circulates, a story who only a few men understand the significance. This mystical idea is not in Gospels, do not penetrate in cathedrals, it is apart from the authority of bishops. Jesus Christ maybe transmitted to Joseph of Arimathea, maybe to several of his disciples, the formula of oral initiation. Those who possessed this formula, this secret, went to the most remote areas of the West, where was released the Roman influence, where there are still forest, lonely places and colleges of men besotted by knowledge.

But a transcendent truth requires for its transmission, souls likely to understand it. An ancient principle of initiations is that each initiated person must find by himself the one that is likely to receive his wisdom.

But instead of disruptions caused by the barbarian invasions, wars, looting of cities, it can happen that the one who seeks a spiritual successor, do not find him.

If the secret word of Jesus was going to disappear! Many men in these times wondered anxiously if the few holders of that word had not obscurely perished. Many have hoped to receive the inheritance and scrutinized for questioning the eyes of the unknown that had knock at night at their door. And of those, those who believed in the existence of an initiation made by Jesus himself, the number decreased considerably.

And among the few that remained in that faith, a new legend circulated. The latest Druidic communities of Ireland and Great Britain knew and practiced the true initiation, which leads man to the divine by an inner path. Merlin the druid had sensed the growing barbarism of the world, the rigor of the dogma, the coming of darkness. He founded an order, organized a mode of transmission, to preserve the flower of the human knowledge.

All these traditions mingled. Those who reported them, mingled them with stories of knights, love affairs with beautiful women in castles. Jesus' initiation materialized in the vase that had collected his blood. Moreover, it is possible that there were two real and also wonderful stories, that of initiation and that of the vase which restrained the blood of Jesus, become miraculous.

The secret of initiation made by Jesus, the supreme substance of his teachings eventually loses its spiritual value and became, in the minds of men, what was connected with his physical form, the spear that had pierced his chest, the cross on which he was nailed, the vase from the meal in Simon's house.

The authors of novels of chivalry, who wrote during the twelfth and the thirteenth century, could not imagine that the ascetic sages gathered by Merlin at the Round Table were anything but warriors, knights with a sword to kill their fellows, and an armor like a shell of insect, for protection. Of those who perpetuated the last word of the science of the teachers and the conquest of the divine in earthly life, they created creatures bristling iron and gleaming steel, men with a strange look of a monster and striving to become metallic.

But it does not appear that this striking transfiguration, this parody mutating the man who seeks God in an anonymous caricature spiked and topped with a plume, ever shocked anyone. I have found nowhere astonishment about it. Everyone has found normal that warriors were grouped by Merlin to be custodians of a sublime secret, coming from the origins of the world, repeated by Buddha and by Jesus. For if the force which spiritualizes to an infinite pain to manifest, the force which materializes is all-powerful. By means of the legend or that of history, by fantasy or truth, symbols are distorted and the spirit is veiled in favor of the material form that represents it.

The history of the essential word bequeathed by the initiate Jesus became the story of a chalice, a spear and a cross. One example will suffice to indicate the direction of the transformation. The cycle of the novels of the Round Table was set by the poet Wolfram von Eschenbrach to whom is commonly attributed a vast and mystical genius. Some even thought that this genius was so powerful that they saw in him the author of all the anonymous epics of Germany[1].

1 Mr. Otto Rahn, a talented young German writer has recently published a very interesting book *La croisade contre le Graal*, but by an ingenious arrangement of citations, it tends to attribute to the German poet Wolfram von Eschenbach almost all mystical poetry of Albigensians, of countries of Toulouse and of Foix î II and also states, with no other proof than his assertion, that there can be no relation between Buddhism and Catharism. Wolfram had obviously not found any. And I could not explain why, in his book on the Pyreneans Cathars, he insists on calling love a "Mine!". His book is still written with love and brings extensive

Well! What supernatural property this belief gives to the Holy Grail when his hero Percival made of it the final conquest? Whenever a girl goes around a room holding the divine vase, a table is suddenly drawn with the most delicious and abundant dishes! The vase containing the blood of Jesus Christ has other miraculous qualities. But this multiplication of food seems the most important.

Thus, the blind have spoken of a beauty that was not accessible to them. But this does not matter! Without sword and without armor, the knights of the spirit continued in the silent forests this quest for the Grail where everyone, according to its degree of perfection, saw a different ideal. And this ideal was for some, the appearance of a lavish meal, and for others the presence of the divine spirit.

documentation.

Bartholomew's lance

Raymond Saint-Gilles, Count of Toulouse was then in charge of the Crusaders and shared this command with the Norman Bohemond and other great lords of France. Each had his knights around him, his prelates and soldiers. They sacked in common but hated each other deeply. It was in Palestine that was born jealousy with no forgiveness, which, a bit later, at the times of the Albigensians, was rushing the northern men, violent and greedy, against the people of Toulouse and the Provence more challenged of mind and of a religious faith less rude.

So the Crusaders, after having taken Antioch, were besieged there in their turn. They were in the grip of famine and of plague appearances. Discouragement came. Hardly if their mutual hatred managed to support them. Horses were eaten. The Ribauds had made feasts of human flesh with the bodies of the dead and it had raised the horror and a mysterious temptation at the same time.

Yet, on a day when Adhémar, bishop of Puy and pope's vicar, was deliberating with the Count of Toulouse and the venerable Pierre d'Hautpoul, a poor priest of Provence who had to give them a surprising communication was introduced among them. This priest, named Peter Bartholomew, was of rustic appearance and of poor knowledge. He had just had a vision of Saint Andrew. This great saint had chosen him. It always appears that superiors of men make strange choices, as if, from beyond, they badly distinguished the different human types. Saint Andrew had led the rude Bartholomew to the church of St. Peter of Antioch, in the heart of the besieged city and had made him glimpse, making the material transparent, under the stones of a certain place of the nave, the lance that had pierced the side of Jesus Christ. After which he ordered him to announce the good news.

A deep skepticism immediately took hold of the soul of the pope's vicar at the same time as an absolute faith possessed that of Raymond,

Count of Toulouse. The account of the wonderful revelation spread throughout the Crusader army and among the inhabitants of the town and the next day a huge crowd gathered around the church of St. Peter of Antioch. Crusade leaders met and decided to practice immediately excavations to verify the assertion of the visionary Bartholomew.

In these heroic times, trickery was feared as strongly as nowadays. Mediumistic characters were also numerous, flattering with false trances and divine imaginary communications. Twelve notables, nobles and priests, were chosen to be judges of the truthfulness of research and make sure that none was duped by any fraud. The church was cleared out and in the presence of the referees began the excavations. One dug all day in the place set by St. Andrew. The pulsating crowd gathered behind the security service. In the evening, there was an excavation of more than seven feet. Nothing had been found. A shudder of disappointment went through the people more and more compact.

Then Peter Bartholomew, probably animated with some new revelation, took off his clothes and ran in his shirt into the pit. He came out of it with the lance. The chaplain of the Count of Toulouse, eyewitness, said he saw the tip of the lance emerge first from the ground and he kissed it. Despite this formal testimony, some chroniclers devoted to the glory of the Norman lords have dwelt on the fact that the visionary of the lance was also the one who had extracted it when it was known that the excavations were inconclusive.

But this urging, injurious for Bartholomew and for the Count of Toulouse himself, only manifested itself later. An immense enthusiasm seized the Crusaders and the people. There were processions, thanksgivings and parties.

Few days later, certain that God had shown himself by a sign, the Crusaders came out of Antioch behind a standard to which the lance was tied and they entirely crushed the Turkish army of Kerbogha. This victory which gave them the possession of a vast country and allowed them to walk on Jerusalem was due to the presence of the divine lance.

The Crusaders left Antioch and the Count of Toulouse gained over his rivals a great prestige by the fact that it was is his camp that the talisman of victory was kept.

From all sides poured offerings as veneration of testimony. Nasty rumors began to circulate, at the instigation of a clergyman called Arnulf, chaplain to the Duke of Normandy. This Arnulf went on all sides, assuring that the lance was a notorious fraud imagined by Raymond of Saint-Gilles, agree with the simple, yet has schemed Bartholomew, to enrich himself with the donations made for the relic.

In terms of miraculous things, doubt has always many supporters and there the doubt was based on the hatred of men of the south. Two camps were formed among the Crusaders and a thousand fights broke out. In the end, Bartholomew offered himself to prove his sincerity and that of the count, by exposing himself to a test of fire. He thus had to expose the truth of the relic and, if unwise, one can deduce from its offer and its insistence to attempt the test, that he was an authentic visionary and not misleading. He prepared himself by fasting for three days.

On April 8, 1099, a large bonfire was prepared in the middle of the Archos camp and fire was set there. Bartholomew then passed amid the blazes, with only his shirt on and the lance in hand.

For what happened to him out of the flame, chroniclers are divided. The crowd, either to determine his condition or to mark him his veneration, fell upon him with such force that he was knocked down and trampled. The knights of the Count of Toulouse were forced to draw the sword to release him. He was taken and nursed. Which injuries? The ones caused by the crowd or the fire?

Some claimed that Bartholomew reproached to himself a little doubt of few seconds he would have experienced before entering the fire, and it is this little doubt that would have probably left some power to the fire, limited power, as it should have normally been consumed.

Peter Bartholomew died twelve days after the test commonly called: God's judgment. Sometimes an ordinary judge do not strictly pronounce himself, leaving pending the trial's outcome. That is what happened. The Crusaders remained divided but the majority continued to believe in the virtue of the relic. The Count of Toulouse continued to carry it with him but we cannot say that it assured him a consistent victory. The walls of Tripoli remained steadfast when he stood to its feet, raising to the sky in his right hand the piece of lance where the eyes of faith could still distinguish under rust, the blood of Christ. Was it not also asking this relic for an unjust power?

The phenomenon of remote viewing undertaking the visionary state of Bartholomew has been nowadays studied, classified and made indisputable. Since the mystical hope of finding Palestine objects that belonged to Jesus or served his punishment, circulated among the Crusaders and was the subject of their talks, it is very possible that a man with psychic gifts detected by sensitive communication, the presence of a metal object buried underground. The huge crowd of Crusaders had to realize a collective sensibility that was able to set in the receptive soul of Bartholomew and make him clairvoyant without any miraculous intervention.

The chroniclers did not give indication on the fate of the lance. It was owned by the Count of Toulouse who jealously kept it with him. But Raymond of Saint-Gilles had renounced to see his city with walls of red brick, bathed by the blue Garonne. Two miles from Tripoli, in Syria, he had built the Citadel of Raymond de Saint-Gilles on the tour from which he looked at the Mediterranean, whose waves, far away on the side of the West, were beating his land and Provencal towns. Seeing death coming, what may have he done of the precious relic, he who only had a young son, to whom he could not confide it? It was probably put next to him in his tomb, as the testimony of the impotence of a relic, so great his miraculous power, to prolong human life.

Joseph of Arimathea

The episode of the lance refers to the material story of the Grail, as the story of the cross and the one of the vase. Everyone knows the story of the cross and that of the multiplication its fragments.

The Empress Helena, mother of Constantine, having returned to Jerusalem, a Jew, hit by inspiration showed her the place where was buried the real cross on which Jesus was nailed. She made it dig out and carried it along with the nails that were used to the torment.

She made of these objects different uses: a nail appeared in the imperial crown, another in the reins of the imperial chariot. Churches of Rome received pieces of the cross. The Empress was sanctified, partly because of the excellence of her distribution. Despite that, it was notorious, almost at the same time, that the real cross, almost entire, was in a church of Jerusalem.

Sarbas, son-in-law of the King of Persia, took hold of it and took it only for simple curiosity, because he adored the sun. He placed it in the residence of Dastagerd, where were massed ancient riches of Persian rulers. The Emperor of Constantinople, Heraclius, who was both skilled general and limited theologian immediately declared war to Khosrow II, King of Persian, to take back the cross. He managed to beat him despite the odds he had to be defeated and captured the sumptuous city of Dastagerd where the historian Theophanes who shared the story of the war, mentions, among fabulous riches of the Arabian nights, the presence of sugar and a little ginger. Heraclius recovered the cross and went to replace it in Jerusalem. But soon after he ran hastily to regain it to secure it in a safe place in Constantinople, because Islamism was threatening.

Something singular happened to the Emperor Heraclius, carrier of the cross. When, followed by his army, he reached Constantinople, he was suddenly possessed by the incapacity to pass the Bosporus. He encamped on the Asian coast and waited. The army encamped around him. Did the true cross did not want to return to Constantinople? Another true cross had yet been brought under Constantine. The Emperor could not see the Bosporus without fainting. His advisers debated and in the end was thrown on the Bosporus a bridge of ships covered by soil and their sides were masked by trees branches so that Heraclius has the feeling to win its capital by crossing a small wood.

For a long time, the emperors of Constantinople had the habit of giving to their daughter or their niece as a wedding gift, a nail or a piece of the true cross. There were, for a very long time, important pieces of it in the Metropolitan Church of Vagharshapat in Armenia, next to a plank from Noah's ark.

The material history of the Grail is primarily the story of the Holy Chalice.

It was during a meal in the house of Simon the Leper, in Bethany, the place of date palms, that Jesus, lifting a vase in his hand, gave the teaching of a rite whose secret meaning is beyond control, but what can only be said it that it is a matter of superior magic of which it is allowed to assume that the essence was related to a mystical union of souls.

At this Simon's house, whose leprosy was on the road to recovery or he accepted as a happy withering of the body, were gathered, besides the twelve disciples, some people who believed in the mission of Jesus. Among them there was Joseph of Arimathea, a man of consideration, a member of the Jewish Sanhedrin, and who remained, for fear of compromising himself, disciple of the outside, that is to say, not devoted.

But a man afraid of compromising himself can suddenly have a revelation which disrupts his life. This is what happened to Joseph.

After that Jesus had been arrested on the Mont of Olives, condemned and crucified, Joseph went to the prefect Pilate to whom he rendered services and regarded him as a person of importance. Simon's house had been sacked by the Roman soldiers and objects that were found were brought back to Pilate as evidence in conviction. Among these objects Joseph saw the vase that Jesus had filled either with wine or a beverage of an unknown composition and asked Pilate for it. This one willingly gave it to him as a gift and additionally granted him permission to take down of the cross Jesus' body and to give it burial.

It was necessary to do it twice. When Joseph went to Calvary with a certain Nicodemus, Jews full of passion prevented him from approaching Jesus. Joseph was obliged to return and meet again Pilate, who gave him some soldiers so that his orders were executed. When Joseph returned to Calvary, a guard named Longinus had just struck Jesus in the side with this lance that was destined for a long fate.

Blood was flowing out of the wound and Joseph collected it in the vase that had served for the ceremony in Simon's house.

Then he carried the body into the grave, on the threshold of which, a time later, Mary Magdalene was to see, among the mists of morning, a man dressed in white, she thought to be the gardener.

There were meetings between the disciples. It appeared to them that what had to be spread around the world was the vital secret which Jesus revealed the depth and with no doubts the means of transmission, the day before his death. This secret, everyone was not able to understand it. He was part of this order of winged knowledge that it is not enough to hear the explanation in words to capture its intimate substance. Maybe of all Simon's guests, so full of the good will of the heart, Joseph of Arimathea was the only one to have received the spiritual legacy, to have been penetrated by the revelatory word.

It is him that the legend designates as going to confines of the Western world known for carrying a vase where he collected the blood, shed by the master at the time of his death.

The object and the blood are only symbols. It is him, Joseph or Arimathea, who has collected this substance of divine order, the thought by which one obtains salvation. He leaves with a chalice under his coat. The precious metal of the chalice is only the miserable dressing-up of man, who is eternally forced to change spirit into matter.

He carries the blood, the pulsating truth, beyond the seas, where the Roman legions stopped their advance, where civilization loses its rights, where old forests still live.

Where there are men seeking the truth, maybe waiting the particular truth of the distant master, who are eager to compare it with theirs. These are the Druids. Since centuries, Druids have in Ireland, their main community. It is towards the Druids that, according to the legend, went Joseph of Arimathea.

How to find his true story under the poems of ignorant poets of the twelfth century. According to them, after lots of adventures, Joseph of Arimathea, accompanied by his family and friends, arrived in the most remote lands of the West. He converts kings, he has many descendants who all become warriors and they deposit the Grail, that is to say a chalice containing the blood of Jesus, in an inaccessible castle. One day, it is announced, a young girl of an inconceivable beauty will be born to one of his grandchildren and she will miraculously give birth to "the one who will know the truth of the Holy Grail."

The secret needed to be announced once more, few centuries later.

The Grail of the Genoese

The capture of Caesarea by the Crusaders of Baldwin, who became king of Jerusalem, and by a group of Genoese that recently landed, was one of the wildest scenes in the history of the Crusades.

The inhabitants of this market town were little trained for war. When they saw shimmering and prancing around their walls, these bristling metallic pyramids of spears that formed the Frank knights, they felt already lost. They sent ambassadors to demonstrate that they have not done anything against the men in iron and that there was no legitimate reason to loot their city and put them to death. The eldest bishop received them and simply explained that the Crusaders "were chosen by God to punish those who went against the law of the Lord."

The town was stormed and its inhabitants slaughtered. The soldiers shared the young women either to the pleasures of the evening or to make them turn hand-mills. "One slit the stomach of Muslims suspected of having swallowed gold. Others were burned in public places to see if their ashes did not contain some bezants. Wicked and perverse population who deserved to die", says a Genoese chronicler.

But the authors of this cruel slaughter of harmless people, apart from the immense riches of the town, received a divine sign, as if a sort of approval was marked to them. The Genoese soldiers found, the chroniclers did not say where, a vase made from a single emerald, an enormous cut emerald and consequently, of incalculable value, containing blood of Jesus Christ. How the blood of Jesus Christ, collected in an emerald which alone accounted for immense wealth, was kept in Caesarea and on what was based the tradition which affirmed it, the chroniclers do not tell it.

In the sharing of the spoils, the marvelous emerald fell to the Genoese, probably offset by a number of young Muslim wives. The Genoese carried it in the cathedral of their city where she was, for centuries, exposed for the veneration of the faithful. The Genoese carried it in the cathedral of their city where it was, for centuries, exposed to the veneration of believers.

Its enormous size surprised in the eighteenth century the mathematician La Condamine. This scientist was tormented by an extraordinary curiosity that drove him to invent clocks and compasses and to circle the world continuously. Visiting the cathedral of Genoa, he pretended to fall on his knees with great pious spontaneity, before the relic. With a quick gesture of his hand fitted with a diamond, he brushed the emerald and he realized that he had scratched it. He concluded that it was of glass.

During the wars of the empire, the French armies stole the emerald in Genoa, as the Genoese had stolen it in Caesarea. It was transported to Paris and experts who examined it, noticed that it was only a large piece of glass where one can still make out the scratch made by La Condamine. The relic was returned without difficulty but was discredited.

It is reasonable to think that it was not the same piece of glass that was originally kept in Caesarea. Muslims had no reason to treasure a worthless item that contained a blood even more worthless in their view. Between 1102, date of return of the Genoese Crusaders in their city and the curious experience of La Condamine, occurred probably a substitution made by a skilled glass cutter that was both a daring thief and maybe an official of the cathedral. The possession of an emerald, unique in its enormity, had to be a powerful object of temptation and had to brave the sacrilege. One can also imagine the aberration of a creature so full of exclusive faith that it wanted to have constantly before its eyes the blood of Christ and stole the relic not for the emerald, but for the blood. But this is part of the things that cannot be known. It will never be known if some selfish dreamer, intoxicated with mystical love, if some strange aesthetic of divine matter did not enjoy in solitude the possession of a priceless treasure especially as it could not be shared with anyone.

The flask of Baalbek

In the book entitled "the supra-normal knowledge" Dt. Osty tells a disturbing story which completes the previous ones.

Everyone knows now what the metagnomy is, a new science which has been studied in recent years, in various countries, more particularly in France, by Dt. Osty. Some people called metagnomists are gifted, in some cases, of a supra-normal power, to detect, by touching an object, events, even very distant, to which the object has participated. Experiments rigorously controlled have shown convincing results.

In 1921[1], Dt. Otsy received, with a view to metagnomistic experiments, a quite confusing photograph that represented a flask hermetically closed whose appearance was that of "a vague ovoid mass" and seemed to contain a liquid.

The person who gave him the photograph was coming back from a study mission in Syria and these are the information it provides about the flask.

It had been found in a necropolis at Kerak, near Baalbek, where were the ruins of the temple of Heliopolis. Mr. Eddet, owner of a wide field had wanted, a few years earlier, to create a magnanery for silkworms. He had made dug deep enough the soil for the foundations. Yet the workers, at a certain depth, found themselves in the presence of a stone used as a door for a vaulted chamber. Moving the stone, they had penetrated in an underground tomb in the centre of which laid a solid gold plate that supported the mysterious flask. Urns were placed symmetrically around the gold plate and the entire tomb gave the impression of having been constructed to shelter the flask.

The urns contained gold coins that workers had seized. But Mr. Eddet had kept the flask. He had it examined by Mr. Maspero who had said that it was a unique piece dating from around Jesus Christ era. On that,

1 The following is resumed according to Dt. Osty's book.

Mr. Edit had photographed and placed it in a bank vault in Beirut.

Yet, Mrs. Morel, Dt. Osty's metagnomist, holding in her hand the photograph of the flask found at Baalbek, made, through her ability of reconstitution, the impressive evocation of a scene from the past.

With broken words, she described a huge temple, a man with a sad face, responsible for thoughts, dominating those around him by the elevation of his intelligence, then crowd noises, the movement of an entire people, strange processions, "as abnormal funeral."

The liquid contained in the flask was, according to her, blood. This blood was that of someone she saw death, far away, by looking back in time. This death moreover, was different from the one we know of Jesus, by the tradition of the Gospels. But it had with it some connections.

The clairvoyant spoke of an entourage of uncultivated forests, a stone house, savage acts, and a neck injury. I quote her description:

"A mountain now… This being is climbing… There is a suffering… He climbs like an arid mountain and is dragging something heavy… So heavy, dark… There is a shock as someone falling. I see around the head, blood. I see men collecting the blood first in something else, and then in this thing I am holding… this travels a lot.

From the above and of the entire account given by Dt. Osty and of which I gave only a brief resume, one can deduce that there is a possibility that the authentic blood of Jesus has been found in an underground tomb near Baalbek. The fact of building an underground vault for a minuscule flask and making it rest on a gold plate is the sign of the importance of this flask. It is necessary to add that when the metagnomist took the photograph and recounted his vision from the past, had no notion of what it was about. She had not even been able to distinguish what the photograph represented exactly.

Dt. Osty tried to buy the precious flask to Mr. Eddet. But apart from Maspero, museums of London and of Cairo had authenticated its age and venerable character. The owner was not able to do the relation between the intrinsic value and its money equivalence. He asked an amount so considerable it made any transaction impossible.

True blood of Jesus, with all the miraculous virtues attached to the blood of an extraterrestrial creature who participated of divine during the life of his body, probably still rests at Beirut, only having for altar the chromed metal of a modern safe; he is next to the soiled wads of bank notes and gold piles of British pounds; he has for a cathedral a modern bank where blow the pestilences of international affairs and this curse eternally attached to wealth.

The Knights of the Round Table

It should be noted that the Church has never attached importance to the history of the Grail, to the journeys of Joseph of Arimathea, nor to the conversion of Great Britain by him. As well as Renan could have made an immense and remarkable history of Christianity, history filled with love smiling for the subject it treated, without saying a word of the Grail.

Here, there is a precious and fertilized indication. If this legend is both neglected by religion and by the most authorized representatives of the religious history, it means that it carries with it a great substance of truth.

This is only a paradox to all appearances. The most important subjects seem to escape to examination. They are never learned in high school and can't be found in textbooks. The same applies for essential questions of metaphysics, the truly gripping questions. One wonder about them alone. The problems of a higher order seem to hover, out of reach, as if they were rebels to written words. Deep down, it is only with oneself that one gets to deal with vital things of the soul.

There is a reality under the legend which represents Joseph of Arimathea carrying to the West a treasure of mystical order. Joseph of Arimathea was going to find Jesus' brothers, the Druids from the communities of Ireland. Was he carrying the good news of the bequeathed secret? Had he the terms of a message to transmit? Was he aspired to find, far from the Jews and Romans also closed to the spiritual word, wise and pure men, teaching the same philosophy as the one who had recently been tortured?

The legend made him reach the distant countries of the West and bequeath to his sons the guard of the Grail who placed it in an inaccessible castle between seven mountains, surrounded by seven precipices, the adventurous castle, within the last northern forests, the treasure remains and is transmitted to those who must receive it.

But the sound of the ax that was making the trees fall gained step by step. The big difference between the Druids and the Christian monks is that one's lived in forests and respected them, pulling from them their wisdom by a magical alliance, whereas the other ones destroyed them, cleared them, and changed them into pastures.

All the legends of saints and monasteries were related to the massacres of trees, to creations of cultures for glorious clearings. Montalembert in his story of Western monks proclaimed with admiration their victory "on the sterile disorder of the spontaneous vegetation". Together with a discipline of land that was plowed, sowed, cut from roads, Christianity was spreading everywhere a discipline of souls. A monk named Pelagius had disturbed the Christianity because he stated that there was no divine grace and that man was free and responsible. The Church trembled on its foundations. What would happen if man dared to believe in his freedom? The bishop Germanus of Auxerre visited twice Great Britain to extract by violence this heresy. But the Anglo-Saxons invaded this country, massacred some of the inhabitants and forced others to shelter in Armorica, the current Brittany.

The legend brings with them Merlin and some Druidic communities since it is in the Brocéliande forest that it places their place of refuge.

The Grail has been forgotten for five centuries and now reappears. Merlin urge the shadow of dark centuries that will spread over the world. The Germanic invasions will spread as layers of lava. The only resistance of the soul will be behind the stone walls of monasteries. But the soul will freeze and die there. The masters of the ancient communities were well aware that the hut of planks and leafs, a direct communication with the forest, is the essential condition to enable man to renew his thought by free food from nature.

The coldness of dogma, the ceremonial of liturgies, will freeze souls.

The sacred treasure must be saved, the treasure which circulates age after age, the treasure of man.

It was then that Merlin established a secret brotherhood, a society of science and soul depositories which will be known under the name of brothers or Knights of the Round Table. Brothers will gather around a table for a meal, because it is during a meal that Jesus has revealed before his death, the sacred rite. The table will be round as a sign of equality because among those who will gather around it, will be men of different classes, warriors, priests, perhaps kings.

The brothers of the Round Table, that the poets of the Middle Ages will call knights, in a time when there is only supremacy for the warrior on horseback, are of total number of forty-nine. But there will be an empty space among them that will make fifty. Why this number? Those who believe in the hidden meaning of numbers and that the world moves by numeral magic will say that fifty is the number of the Holy Spirit[1].

On the empty seat was supposed to sit the one who would have found the Grail. The Grail was not lost. It was resting, emerald heart with matte shades where boils the living blood of the soul, in the mysterious room, always closed, of the initiation.

This room was located perhaps in one of these doorless and windowless towers that was found in Ireland and which astonished the archaeologists, because it seemed at first sight that no form could penetrate it, no physical form at the very least. This room was maybe elsewhere, between the four underground stones of an anti-druidic dolmen, between the trunks of four oaks of the Brocéliande forest. This room only needed to be long as a man's body, so that the disciple rested there during his three-day journey in the afterlife.

The fiftieth guest was the one who had found the Grail, the one who by his inner virtue had reached the enlightenment, had, in his living body, discovered the path of the spiritual world where stay pure souls. To walk this path, one would have to be detached, courageous and chaste. The impure and proud who tended to lay his hands on the Grail without being worthy of it, had his legs pierced by a magical lance, which was the symbol of the inability to walk henceforth on the path, behind which was his punishment. Thus, it happened to the imprudent king

---

1 See on the subject, *Le Secret de la Chevalerie* by Victor Emile MICHELET. Furthermore Philo of Alexandria, speaking of Therapeutes, said: fifty is the holiest and most natural number of all, composed of the power of the right-angled triangle, source of birth of all things.

Mordrain.

But the winner of the great temptation of lust, of the power to generate new earthly men, whether named Galahad or Percival, this one reached the divine Grail and would sit among his brothers. He knew the secret. He, from the human kingdom, he had reached the soul.

Then the bread was broken and the wine circulated among the insiders. Fifty men were very little, in the middle of this wild West, where, later on, the emperor Charlemagne, enacting the death penalty against cannibalism, enacted it in the same time against those who ate meat during Lent.

This seems very little and it was a lot. If in India, men who stand out from the chain of meanings are numerous, if they are seen, sitting along roads and if they inhabit monasteries, it should be considered that India is the chosen land where blew, as far as history allows us to see, a beneficial force pushing the souls to the contemplation of spiritual things. Jesus in Palestine could gather only twelve disciples. Had Pythagoras much more of them? The West, at the time when Druids were going to disappear, was becoming the bad side of the planet.

The fifty brothers of the Round Table, the so-called knights, went out of the Brocéliande forest and scattered in the world where they would no longer be talked about for a long time. All authors of novels of chivalry who took them as heroes of their war adventures, their fabulous tales, seem to have ignored the mystical meaning of the Grail. They portray Merlin's companions as men with big bright swords whose blows split into two the enemy knight, whatever the temper of his armor and the embonpoint of the person. Yet, they knew that, more than the courage, chastity is necessary for these heroes of an ideal of which they have no idea. The possession of the secret includes chastity, because chastity has a close relation with the secret. The spiritual creator must not be a flesh creator. Whoever finishes the human race by the return to the divine must not contradict his work, leaving behind him an incarnate son who would have to undertake the same quest.

Neither Robert de Boron, nor Chrétien de Troyer, nor Wolfram von Eschenbach say expressively what the Grail is. They did not know. The legend has been mysteriously whispered, it was told in the evenings, it is not known where it was born, or who was the first to tell it. The very etymology of the word Grail is uncertain. The most likely is the one that wants the Grail to be a derivative of gresal, which in the Oc language meant vase and still has this meaning today in the Frenchified patois, spoken in Toulouse[1]. The legend must have been born almost everywhere. Its origin is usually placed in Great Britain or among the Celts of Armorica. Yet, Wolfram von Eschenbach assured to have received it from a Provençal poet called Kyot or Guiot who himself would have held it from a Jew of Toledo called Flégelantis. No trace was found of this Guiot and in a unanimous way, scientists who weigh the truths and the lies, stated that this Guiot had never existed and that Wolfram von Eschenbach had invented him to give weight to his work! Has anyone ever seen a poet flattering himself of holding its subject of someone else and modestly hedging before the name of a stranger?

The Grail shone almost everywhere. In the darkness of ignorance, those who have suffered of the dogmatic narrowness of religion, of the absence of reasonable hypothesis on man's destiny, those who have lamented of not knowing how to hope, had in their worst hours the consolation that there was throughout the world few men more favored than them, who knew and transmitted between themselves the repository of knowledge. Violence reigned supreme, there were no books, no philosophical teachings and evil was growing. Yet, somewhere shone the light of salvation[2].

---

1 Throughout my entire childhood I called a vase a gresal.

2 This is the most likely hypothesis. In the eleventh century, the largest school of philosophy and poetry in the world was a Jewish school in Toledo. This city also had a group of insiders, attracted by the freedom of thought that prevailed there.

Montségur

There are places on earth which are predestined. Varanasi, Delphi, Lourdes are among them. The reasons of this predestination are numerous. Those who visit these places sometimes say that they feel presences. The accumulation of the thought of the pilgrims, their wishes and their prayers, could have condensed into things. Certain trends of a particular nature, similar to those which Mr. Lakhovsky have recently measured, perhaps come out of the earth. The spirit blows there and it is given to some to be touched by it.

In the mountains of Ariège, after the gothic towers of Foix, after the singing of Pyrenean torrents in the narrow valleys, after the piling up of the slate schist with bluish reflections, stands the shrine of Montségur or Monsalvat.

Monsalvat because there was a time when those who went and died there were saved.

Of all times, this side of the earth was consecrated to the mind. Dolmens still half buried confirm that it was a place of worship long before the Druids. On top of a nearby mountain, Saint-Bartholomew, the archeologist J. Mandement[1] has found a Celtiberian station, which was then used by Phoenicians and Greeks. The Druids stayed there, but as elsewhere, their plank huts under the trees did not leave marks. If Montségur was chosen by Esclarmonde de Foix, to be the foundation of the castle where had to shelter the Perfect Albigensians and the last lovers of the divine wisdom, is that there was in the breast of his clay and the heart of its stones, an inexplicable supra earthly breath that gave them a taste of their spiritual homeland.

This relates to the Albigensian drama of the eighteenth century when the Church, with its chivalry, its judges and its bonfires, destroyed the

---

1 See the series of these well-documented articles in the newspaper *La* Dépêche for more details.

last spurt of the Southern soul.

The inquisition had settled in all the cities and all the castles had been taken from Rhône until the pines of Aquitaine. The Albigensian church had become so secret that many doubted his existence. Those who believed contained their faith in them. Denunciation reigned supreme. The Albigensians who took refuge in the forests of the Pyrenees were hunted liked wild beasts.

One castle still resisted, it was Montségur. Thirty years earlier, Esclarmonde de Foix, in anticipation of the misfortunes that would overwhelm his coreligionists, had developed it for a long resistance. The mountain was pierced by galleries where were piled up provisions for a long siege. There were underground rooms to pray and vaults for tombstones. The towers were separated from the valley by a spiral of three thousand steps.

The old count Raymond de Péreille had gathered in this refuge the members of the Cathar church et the perfects who remained. He thought he could brave on the distance, close to the sky, the armies of the king and the pope.

He was wrong. Montségur was taken and its defenders massacred. I have recounted at length in other books[1] and I speak of it here only about the Grail. A legend says that the Grail, the Grail of Joseph of Arimathea, the emerald chalice with the miraculous blood of Jesus, was transported to Montségur.

If a mystic talisman was kept somewhere by faithful and pious men, inheritors of the true tradition of Jesus, it is likely that in the uncertainty of times, these guardians thought of carrying their treasure in the place where it would be more secure. All the Christianity knew that there was in the mountains of Ariège, an unassailable castle where men animated by the primitive faith found refuge.

The initiated brothers of the Round Table, the Druids inheritors of Merlin, marched towards this favored land of the South, towards the Pyrenees where sheltered from the torrents and chasms, between the long stone corridors, principal forests still lived and where brotherhoods

1 See *Magiciens et illuminés* and *Le sang de Toulouse*.

of Druids had to shelter in inaccessible retreats.

The thought that Montségur could escape to the growing evil, the cruelty of men, the ruthless ferocity of the Church for what it called execrable heresy. An army commanded by the Seneschal of Carcassonne, had enveloped the mountain. War machines overcame the solidity of the towers, and one night, after months of siege, the royal troops forced its walls.

But what was called the treasure of the Cathars, real treasure, which was supposed to contain all the riches of Albigensian lords, transported for thirty years in this place of security, the treasure of the Cathars was already gone.

Raymond de Péreille, sensing the disaster, took it out one night, thanks to the betrayal of some guard soldiers in the valley. Led by the Cathar bishop Raymond de Saint-Martin, the treasure reached the forests of the next mountains and was transported, as it is said, in the Ornolac cave. If the Grail was at Montségur, it left that night without moon, among the guardians whose horses had hoofs wrapped in sheet, behind the old silent bishop as a ghost, towards the forests of Belestar, where trees tented protective arms.

Anyhow, if it had not left with bishop Raymond de Saint-Martin, the defender of Montségur Pierre Roger had the possibility to take it with him. The terms of the surrender allowed him to leave with the soldiers of the siege, his physician, his architect, and the furniture and treasures of the castle.

If the Grail was at Montségur, what had it become after the fall of the castle? Perhaps had it been buried in Ornolac when the Albigensians, who took refuge there, were walled up in this cave. Perhaps had it been taken elsewhere by those who had its guard. One spoke of the Château de Saissac[1] in the black mountain, and of the one in Cucugnan, on the road to Perpignan. J. Mandement has ventured a hypothesis that it could

---

1 I interviewed the writer Dupuy Mazuel who is the owner of the Château de Saissac. He knew nothing of the presence of the Grail at his place. It was the treasure of the Visigoths kings who, according to vague assurances, was hidden in his domain, he told me. But he had not searched for it yet. This is a beautiful negligence! Old castles are full of treasures. They only have to be found.

have been transported in the Château de Montréal, which belonged to the Hospitallers.

What is certain is that it left Monségur and the fanciful researchers who shake for some time now the mountain by pickaxes will not find it nor will find the treasure of the Cathars. Likewise, the tombstones that they will be able to discover in the underground galleries will only contain dust of bones.

As Druids, the Albigensians made it a rule to despise gold and never adorn themselves with jewelry. The carnal corps was unimportant and could not be recovered by any ornament.

* * *

When Percival just discovered the Grail, Middle Ages storytellers say that he goes with it to heaven where it remains in a kind of magical expectation. But another tradition wants him to go with it to Prester John.

Prester John was the king and the great pontiff at the same time, of the kingdom of the Keraites, behind Armenia and Persia. A colony of Nestorians once came in this country and had Christianized it. All sorts of fabulous tales ran in the West about Prester John. It symbolized far away, towards the West, a mysterious and Christian India. The pope Alexander III sent him an ambassador at the end of the twelfth century, and it is not known why he chose a physician, what could make assume that among the things that made Prester John famous, there was the weakness of his health.

By making the Grail leave for Prester's John India, poets of the Middle Ages send it back to its initial homeland. It is only in the mountains of Himalayas that wise men find a certainty of human peace. It is from there that left the first missionaries and where they return once the mission is accomplished or when, by the fact of the hardness of souls to which it was intended, it could not be fulfilled. The same tradition for the Rosicrucians is found in the eighteenth century.

The spiritual descendants of the fifty brothers of the Round Table set off perhaps towards the mountains of solitude and of preparation for life. In virtue of a rhythm one ignores, there are times where the message is brought and others where men continue to struggle in the shadows. It is only a little later that Tsongkhapa established the principal that every century, there would be an attempt to bring the spiritual light to the West. The Grail returned periodically from the distant East, and everyone could contemplate it to the extent of one's ability to see. But the modern Percival did not have to lift the veil to show the eternal treasure. It passed anonymously. No one has recognized or asked for it.

The spiritual Grail

The true Grail has no material existence. It is a secret related to death. It is a secret which has to do with the eternal life of the soul. This secret was taught by Jesus at the time when this master felt he was going to die. Perhaps was he only understood by Joseph of Arimathea and the simple and pure men who were Jesus' disciples have only retained the verbal appearance and neglected the deeper meaning.

The secret of the Grail is the one of the communication with the divine spirit and consequently the liberation of earth.

Before Jesus, Buddha had discovered it alone in his meditation under the fig tree and had taught it under a different form. Even though this secret is of such order that, for it to be accessible, one must have penetrated a higher spiritual level than the one where men usually move, one can say that the Buddhist form of salvation is individual, whereas the one taught by Jesus had a character of collective union.

The evangelists, voluntarily or not, have only reported the material events of the life of Jesus, they left aside any doctrine. There is no doubt that Jesus has given an explanation of the world and taught what happens to men after death. Even to the lowest degree of simplicity, these are the explanations the listeners are waiting for. Jesus had to satisfy them by trying to adapt his words to the mentality of those who listened. As simply he had spoken, his doctrine, when it had to be reported by well-intentioned men but ignorant, was altered and rendered incomprehensible. The evangelists thought that what they could do best was to remove any attempt of explanation on this subject and to confine themselves to stories and parables likely to enthrall.

They are uncertain and fast when it comes to relating the essential revelation of Jesus during the meal at Simon's. One cannot take their account to the letter in an absolute way. It is important to retain the general thought crystallized in the word union or communion, or the merger of souls and in the symbolic representation of the flesh and blood under the appearance of bread and wine.

Before dying, Jesus has revealed a mystery of the spiritual life. Can it be more important, than the real purpose of man, that of his perfection? The ideal of the wise is not happiness, it is becoming more perfect, to aspire to a higher state of existence which, furthermore, leads him indirectly to happiness. To reach this state one must be transformed, born again, receive life.

The one who received life, escapes the chain of lives, the movement of rebirths, the trap of incarnations where there is no progress because of the terrible law that impels the man to fall asleep in his pleasure and leaves him at the time of death as mediocre as the minute he was born in the flesh.

But this is the supreme difficulty, the mysterious passage from one kingdom to another, so mysterious that the insiders have only talked about it in sanctuaries where they celebrated the mysteries. The modern scientists do not believe the possibility of this passage. They are more or less unanimous in saying that man is the last stage of the evolution of creatures and that it is impossible to probe the future.

In order to get closer to the mystery which is in the secret, to grasp the nature, it is possible to use an analogy. Still few years ago, science was passionately seeking for the spontaneous generation. The point of debate was to know if, having sterilized matter in a closed vase and killing by a high temperature all the living organisms that were contained there, life could arise of itself. The problem was to know whether the inorganic matters one supposed dead (they were in fact, at a slower degree of the existence) could spontaneously become organic, that is to say extract from their own immobile substance, this mysterious spouting the moving life is.

After many experiments, it definitely seemed to demonstrate that there was no spontaneous generation.

The passage of stone to plant remained a mystery. Science could analyze the physical laws of the inorganic world; it could inspect by biology of what was organic and animated. But this science remained silent on the meeting of the two worlds. There was a contact point that it could not determine. There was a strange transformation whose data was rebellious to all knowledge.

In the physical world, life do not arise of itself. The seed of life needs to be brought so that life can develop. But the laws are the same everywhere and have correspondences from one world to another, from physical to spiritual.

Between the mineral and vegetal there is a separation as profound as a gulf and an ignored cosmic law yet wants this gulf to be crossed. Between the human state and a following state, there is a gulf as deep and the cosmic law which progresses with certainty, even if it is eyeless and wrapped in a shroud of darkness, must use the same method to establish the contact point from one state to another.

Just as was needed for the dead matter to become alive, an external input of the seed of life, just as for the man to become divine and it must receive a spiritual contribution, be fertilized by a seed of mind.

This fertilization is only effective if it is exercised over men prepared by a long training, on disciples already detached of the forms of terrestrial life. But how is it practiced, what secret path takes the seed to descend in the abyss of the soul, of what nature is this seed, this has always remained the most unfathomable mystery that man has to decipher.

Men of genius are those who have, in virtue of an unknown law, a partial descent of the mind. A beam of illumination have touched them. Jesus knew the secret of making this beam of illumination permanent and making it pass death. Sensing his close death, he has hastily revealed it, probably with the regret of not having around him, disciples prepared enough to understand it. He has thrown that seed in an uncultivated land where it might not fructify. The experiment was supposed to give reason to this fear.

"No one, if one do not rise of the spirit, shall enter into the kingdom of God, for what is born of the flesh is flesh."

The preparation was to be made by the abandonment of all that is earthly, family, wife, children, and the disciple who needed to bid farewell to his family before devoting himself to the ineffable, for this too human thought that was the farewell, became unworthy of the ineffable. It was necessary not to have any involvement with the world, renounce, turn the other cheek. Then one became "God's wheat", the true disciple, ready for the realization of the promise.

But it is then that had to intervene a transcendent experiment. Which one exactly? There are fugitive echoes of it in certain words of the Gospels. "That they all may be one...To be one..." is frequently found in Jesus' mouth. And this experience led to a steady state where the cycle of incarnations was over and which was what they call either God's kingdom or eternal life.

Buddha has taught before Jesus, a similar secret. He has taught, with the four truths, that there was for man only one important concern, which was to escape to the terrestrial sorrow and enter Nirvana.

Buddha's Nirvana is the equivalent of God's kingdom of Jesus. But on those transcendent stays, neither of them have given any details. These great founders of religion on the word of which humanity has lived, have advised men to renounce to the safe land, to participate in a world that they did not want to describe!

Perhaps they have not done so because they could not, this world being indescribable in words. Maybe they have done it with precious details, priceless indications to chosen disciples and these conversations having not been written down, were lost.

But the Hindu and neo-Platonic philosophies, mystics of the Middle Ages with their ideal pursuit of the divine world, allow the one who tries to understand them, to catch a glimpse of the light behind the cloud. There is a cloud for each school, a cloud for each mystic, but the light is the same.

It is possible to represent by analogy the human condition in Nirvana or in God's kingdom.

There are very few minutes in the ordinary man, where ideas move more faster, where they call others in, where one have in the mind something like a fraternity of active ideas. This can be produced by the discovery of a problem, the accession to an artistic conception of which one had dreamed about without reaching it. It is an euphoria of knowledge, the participation in a broader field of knowledge.

There are other minutes, more frequent in the ordinary man, where one can feel a more emotional than spiritual desire to mingle with all the beings, to be closely united with them. This form of desire begins with love for one person, but takes in this limited love a point of reference which allows him a broader form of love.

There is a love euphoria similar to the knowledge euphoria, more common and more easy, because of the physical part of which it drags its origin.

Both euphoria give a taste of what a greater intoxication can be, that would participate in both of the two. In imagining what one feels in the highest moments of his existence, is only an imperfect and dull reflection of a more brilliant light, multiplying the force of the aspiration and perfect joy in which one swims, one can represent to oneself the ecstatic state, subtle, the donation state, the receiving state, the state of communion that must be the Nirvana of Buddha and God's kingdom of Jesus.

In what measure one is led there by the solitary contemplation and by the absolute detachment? Is there an hour of the life, where just as the fruit falls from the tree because it has reached a point of maturity, the soul detaches itself from earthly things and falls of itself in the Nirvana? But there are fruits that rot on the tree under any delusion, of a lack of audacity, of a beatitude of immobility. For those ripe fruits, as for young fruits eager to be mature before time, Buddha and Jesus have formulated a rule.

By the removal of the desire that man can solitarily exercise, one reaches Nirvana. The fruit detaches by itself.

Jesus' method is different. He shakes the tree. The fruit comes off early.

The secret of this method contained the union of a group of men, of a mystical association whose members dragged their power from the spiritual substance of their fraternity. The mystery by which surrounded themselves early Christian communities seem to attest, however if these communities were initiated in the supreme mystery. When these communities became the Christian church, and had to take on the task of a great ecclesiastical organization, the divine secret lost all value, it turned into sacraments accessible to crowds, his meaning altered and his understanding was lost.

It can be found in the twelfth century among the Albigensians.

The Albigensian doctrine held both Buddhism and early Christianity. Buddhism was brought to it by the Bulgarian Nicetas and his disciples; early Christianity had always lived of a secret life, next to churches too loaded with gold, too opulent convents. The Albigensians united the involution in matter taught by Buddhism and fall out of the sky of early Christianity. For them the man was to join the Buddhist atman or the heavenly angel of the Christians, and the two were one. The world was a dark passage one had to cross, a hell one could escaped by becoming first a Perfect and by receiving then the Consolamentum.

Being perfect was only a preparatory state.

It is by the Consolamentum that one received salvation.

The essence of the Consolamentum, remained hidden. Only the formulas of ritual are known and Ton knows that it included a meeting with purified men. The spiritual contribution, the divine seed was given by a Perfect who already possessed it. He transmitted the life of which he was the depositary. A kiss was the symbol of the received gift and the kiss was circulating among believers who were present as the visible sign of the current of love that passed from one to another.

The Consolamentum was Jesus' secret, the spirit of the Grail.

At a certain degree of height, the great mysteries meet. What has been called the secret of chivalry, the platonic love of the knights of the Middle Ages, has something to do with the Grail. The Troubadours sang it without fully understanding it. But some had to know the mysterious rite of lovers, rite taught since thousands of years in some sects of India.

The meeting of the two loves at their supreme degree of realization produced the transcendent flame by which one is projected into the region of the mind. Nature has the same laws everywhere, and the upper alchemy finds examples in lower realms. Two stones that one hit produce a spark. Of the combined effort of two human souls springs fire. The lovers, by a communion that they have to discover, can realize the divine. In the Albigensian Consolamentum, it was the Perfect who was the transmitter of love from love that he drew from the depths of his being. The approach of the lips was the communion of breaths, symbolized the realization.

The fact that this achievement was accomplished by the love of two beings who went from the physical love to arrive at perfect love, or that it needed an enlightened being, a man having the power to store love and pass it on, it is certain that it was known and practiced during the Middle Ages.

Has it passed with the persecutions of the church or has its transmission only been more secret? In what measure has it been known to the Rosicrucians, Albigensians heirs? Is there today in the West a spiritual son of the Druid Merlin and of the Albigensian Raymond de Saint-Martin, owner of the divine word and likely, by making it resonate, to break the hard doors of the souls?

The mystery of the joyful death

The Grail was in its inner essence a method to attain perfection and therefore a method to die wisely.

No people could better understand it than the one that had been raised by the Druids in total disregard of death, who knew by themselves how necessary it is to die with ease and joy.

Because it is our conception of death, the development of the animal terror, which has skewed the doctrine. It has nothing desperate and it can even be considered as the greatest manifestation of the love of life as it allows an undefined extension of life in more perfect conditions. The meal at Simon's was not a meal of despair. The assimilation made by Jesus of the bread and wine to his flesh and his blood has a close relation with Buddha's communion in nature, among the trees of the forest, when he meditated on the salvation of men, communion which must correspond to an unimaginable degree of joy.

The ideal of perfection, the death considered as a single pass, does not exclude the terrestrial joy, on the contrary. The detachment is a way of joy that allows to reach a better state. It does not only contain a promise. The detachment is the first necessary step and it has in itself its reward. A desire can be abandoned as a burden. Everything depends on the truthfulness of the abandonment. In a way, the detachment is a new possession. The communion with things and with the souls of men only begins when one is detached. But one cannot in this domain, act as a greedy man in life, saying: give and take, to abandon on one side only to cease on the other.

The possession of the divine world can only be obtained by an act of faith. First, it is necessary to abandon

the terrestrial world to see coming forward the divine world. The man must make the first step.

Nowadays, the meaning of the Grail is cleared, the true understanding of death is lost. It inspires terror instead of arising hope. But it took a long time for the cessation of the ancient Druidic spirit, the wisdom of the man in front of death.

The whole history of the Middle Ages confirms that it still subsisted there. One has only to think of the selflessness that inspired the artists of the cathedrals, the perfection of the work they reached, to the scruple that pushed them to make them perfect, even the parts that no one could see. They striped themselves of their artistic pride. They sacrificed it to the divine. Small sacrifice because everything confirms, especially the splendid laughter of few stone faces on the pediment of the basilicas, that they were joyful men. Just like the perfect serenity, the obedience to destiny which is seen in the features of their saints, shows that they must have had in their souls what they passed on to the stone. They had to make of death the same joyful idea as their ancestors, the Gauls. They were detached. They had sacrificed their personality to the group to which they belonged. They thought life all the more beautiful they could come out of it more easily.

It is the lack of faith or rather the lack of knowledge that has caused the despair before death. If it is only a question, as the Bhagavad-Gita say it "to leave old cloths in order to wear new ones" that is to say to enter in new bodies, death is a change of little importance. It is a question of leaving a physical state where everything is weight, limitation and pain, to move to a state of active thinking and living love, death is a desirable thing one must await with impatience.

Few indications allow to think that it happened to some men to use the force of union that came from a group, to die with serenity and reach a higher state.

A crypt was found in the black mountain, not far from Carcassonne, skeletons dating of the Albigensian era. "They were lying in a circle, heads in the centre, feet in circumference, like the spokes of a perfect wheel."

Yet in the recent excavations made in the Téviec island, along the coasts of Brittany, have also been found skeletons whose disposition was shaped like a circle. This circle was regular and led to think of some funeral rite.

But the age of the skeletons were esteemed to have five thousand years.

Those who have stretched out there to die in a secret loneliness, and have drawn with their bodies a geometrical figure of a wheel, have continued this strange and so unusual purpose at the time of death only because it was a rite of an extreme importance and of which they waited a sublime result.

If the result of the excavations in Téviec is correct, the knowledge that had the Albigensians of a certain way of dying was possessed by peoples who lived five thousand years ago and who maybe were the ancient Atlanteans.

If it is necessary to give a name to this secret of the wise, to this secret which probably flows since the beginning of the world, the one that suits it best is the secret of the joyful death.

From the moment Ton has changed the idea that one has of death, one became a new man. The highest wisdom of life is to create for oneself a force of communion strong enough with men and with all living creatures in order to be able at any places and at any time, to feel united with them. The separation exists on earth at its absolute degree. The union is made with the loss of the body, or rather can be achieved by it if one is prepared. Death is then a happy event, the release from the prison of which Plato spoke, a liberation. It has to be considered as a subject of joy.

But the reason for this joy, everyone has to make its discovery. Everyone has to give rise in oneself to the blood emerald of the inner Grail.

THE SECRET OF TAROT

The 78 bones of the truth

The history of the origins of life give astonishing teachings. One learns that nature, with a foresight to unlimited views and a concern shown every second, watched over his creations so that they are perpetuated, according to its primitive will.

Thus "there is an evident relation between the number of eggs laid and the dangers to which they are exposed. Fish whose eggs float, exposed to countless enemies, produce much more than others. The cod has over nine million of them, the plie rude has more than three hundred thousand of them[1], etc..."

Nature having taken decisions required that they be executed. It wanted the cud and the plie rude to split the waters of the Arctic seas, and it added them an exceptional faculty of egg production.

What nature does in the material domain of marine species must have a correspondence in the domain of its superior creations.

It must protect with the same vigilance the germination of spiritual eggs. So that they are not eaten by their enemies more numerous and voracious than those of cods and plie rudes, it must employ a certain process of survival.

It is curious to observe that despite the astonishing difference in areas on where the process is carried out, it remains more or less the same. One has to remember the ancient principle: what is above is like what is below.

As the races multiplied on earth, they sank more and more into the love of life with the elements that gave them physical matter, but the communication with the higher world could not be lost. It was necessary that at some point of time, in the darkness where he had penetrated, the man could relight the lamp and find the path towards the light. Yet, the words die with those who heard its syllables. The manuscripts are eas-

1 Louis Vialleton:*L'origine des êtres vivants.*

ily destroyed and even the signs engraved on stone crumble with time.

Of what incorruptible form, of what purified iron, of what marble with eternal atoms would therefore cover themselves the essential truths, in order to be transmitted through the depths of ignorance?

The first initiators of humanity charged the humane passion to spread by itself the immortal intelligence that is supposed to come at the end of ages.

The first initiators of humanity made the human passion responsible to spread itself, the immortal intelligence needs to be able, at the end of the ages, to destroy this passion with the inexorable ray of his burning mirror. They made a game, a game with pictures and figures, a game that could entertain children, a game where the common man could satisfy his taste for lucre by having fun, where the one who had intuitions could exercise himself by guessing the future, where the one tormented by the secret of things could find the solution of great enigmas, laws of nature, the mystery of death.

Because the guiding laws by which the world was created, these laws some of which are known of men, and others are still ignored, have been enclosed in Tarot and the one who would have a thorough knowledge of it would penetrate the truths still veiled for human reason.

So that eternal science floats like a buoy through the centuries, the early wise, they know neither the name, or the origin, nor the physical appearance, painted pictures, colored pictures, related to the laws of numbers and those of colors, representative images and symbols they launched across the world, certain that what is attached to pleasure cannot perish.

And they were right. The first signs have been painted on barks and then on metal strips, on ivory, on parchments, on leather and later on, on simple cardboards. Colors erased themselves, the numeral thread has been blurred; the illuminators have changed according to the times the shape of things reproduced and the customs of characters. A key was lost, a key from which were supposed to come out several keys, according to the spiritual, passionate or physical world that was questioned, a key that many have greedily claimed to recover and to whom the persistence of their ignorance had proven wrong. But Tarot has crossed the persecutions of churches, the widespread destructions, the witch trials; it had braved Saul's word, the eternal Jewish and Christian rage. "The seers and visionaries should be punishable by death!". Tarot came to us, processed, injured, lame, but with its secret dynamism, its vital signs.

They are like a skeleton stripped by the avidity and the foolishness of men, the skeleton of the lost wisdom. This wisdom once existed as an entity in the minds of wise men who had its deposit. It died and only remains 78 bones of it.

The paleontological science reconstitutes in their whole integrity beings, who have lived a hundred thousand years ago just by finding on a land a fragment of a heel and a frontal bone splinter. With these minimal fragments it makes plesiosaurs with lizard head or toothless megatheriums live in front of us. It is up to paleontologists the idea to resurrect the truth with the 78 bones of its 78 members painted on cardboard.

The great antiquity of Tarot

Everyone knows what Tarot is, a deck of 78 cards, including two degrees. The first level consists of 22 cards called the major arcana and the second by 56 cards, the minor arcana. These cards are covered with figures which are symbols.

Their great age is immense. If Court de Gébelin have assigned them the age of the Egyptian civilization and if, with Etteilla he made of it the book of Thoth Hermes, it is because at their time the thought of India and China were still ignored and that their inhabitants were only designated by missionaries with general names of pagans or gentiles. It is furthermore astonishing to think that it is barely from one century that we have in Europe the knowledge of the Vedas, and also of the oldest monuments of the human wisdom, understanding how limited!

Similarly, Éliphas Lévi has seen a connection between the number 22 of the major arcana and the 22 letters of the Hebraic alphabet. He judged this decisive match, has assigned a letter to each major arcana and declared that Tarot was the book of the sacred wisdom of ancient Hebrews. But Vaillant, in his untraceable book *Histoire vraie des vrais bohémiens* [True story of the true bohemians] has shown that the root of each word translating each symbol of major arcanas approached as much to the Sanskrit as to Hebrew.

There is an Indian Tarot dating back to ancient times and a Chinese Tarot Vaillant has described, established with the same combinations of the number seven. It has the appearance of a table and it dates back to "the early stages of the Chinese empire, the period of the making of the zodiac. It is in every instance, prior to Moses."

Who is the inventor of the first Tarot? Was there a unique inventor or is it the work of a community of wise? The most plausible hypothesis is that Tarot was composed by the first initiators of humanity, those who guided men to the beginning of time and that a legend, without evidence of course, brought from another planet to put on earth the seeds of mind.

Chinese encyclopedias place at the beginning of the organization of their country, superhuman personalities that have human heads but have kept the bodies of primitive snakes. Tarot has not the age of these fabulous creatures. But it could have been composed by this Fo-hi who takes part in historical times, to whom Confucius has attributed the invention of writing and who has left a book of divination, the Y-king of which we possess a translation, despite its great old age.

Hindu Pouranas are full of legends relating to large beings endowed with very extensive spiritual powers and who live in a mysterious city on Mount Meru, or this Shambhala, fantastic city, that travelers in the Gobi Desert, thought to have got a glimpse of at the edge of a lake with supernatural mirages.

Tarot may have been the work of the initiator Melchizedek of whom only the name almost came up to us, but whose name has kept the power.

"He is the leader of those who came from other heavens and he has no ancestors on earth. His body was not born of a woman. It was created by the will of his possessor, directly[1]."

Melchizedek is mentioned in the Bible as king of Salem, identified in Jerusalem and it was he who first made the use of the bread and wine in a priestly ritual.

It is possible to recall about him a passage of the visions of Anne Catherine Emmerich. When it comes to legendary stories which only rely on extremely vague data, the testimony of some visionaries brings a relative authenticity to the facts but which becomes stronger as the observation stands on the plan of intuition.

Anne Catherine Emmerich describes in the thrilling landscape of an arid Palestine, under an anterior light to first migrations, a man dressed in white or rather a man's silhouette she recognizes to be Melchizedek. He touches the slope of mountains. He listens to the whisper of the ground waters. He seeks solitude in the appropriate place for the birth of sources. She sees him piercing granitic masses with something long

1 G.E. Monod Herzen. Article from *Le Lotus Bleu* 1926.

and luminous, a ray gifted of the power to pass through the matter.

Tarot was also attributed to Enoch who would be the author of books previous to Moses, one of them, *Le livre des batailles de l'Eternel* is so ancient that with him Genesis is seen as modern writing.

Tradition attributes to Enoch a life of 365 years, a figure which suggests that he was the inventor of astronomy and arithmetic, the idea of his age remaining linked in the minds of men to the one of the movement of the earth around the sun, of which he would have been the first to make the calculation.

The Bible, about his death does not use the word it employs to notify the end of other Patriarchs, words which are:"And he died". It said: He was withdrawn to God. Because Enoch, according to tradition, did not die but disappeared. It is likewise for some legendary heroes. No one witness their death. Which means that the man who reaches in his lifetime the divine spirit escapes to the phenomenon of death, the merging with the mind when it is absolute, bringing an absolute destruction of the body.

Enoch, great grand-father of Noah, announced the flood and it was perhaps the prescience of this cataclysm that led him to summarize the essential knowledge for the human development in simple symbols.

As everyone has confirmed it by repeating the assertion of his predecessors, Tarot cards might have been the work of Thoth Hermes, the father of the magus, the one on whose behalf one has reported all the knowledge of the Egyptian civilization and of which Iamblichus has still been able to see in Alexandria the ten thousand books which are attributed to him.

But Tarot could also be the work of several wise men living in distant countries and at different times. These wise, starting from the same raw data, that is to say, knowing the figures underlying the laws of the world, they managed to attain, mathematically, numbers 22 and 78 of the Tarot and the same sequence of symbolic images. These images, under the transcendent mathematical ideas, have imposed themselves for themselves. There is probably only one possible combination whose mixture is capable of generating all combinations of the mind.

Thus, in virtue of a decision of this unique centre of which we know nothing but of which we can here and there find the traces of some filiations, the secret book, the book where are the laws of nature, has come up to us, the result of a vast theorem whose total solution may only be given at the end of earthly times.

The curse related to Tarot

What is most striking when studying the work of wise and conscientious men who have studied Tarot to explain it, is that these men are positive or in love with mystery, is a special dizziness, a kind of very special exhilaration which is, I believe, proper to the study of symbols.

The symbolism seems linked to a particular disorder of the reasoning faculty which makes find analogies where there is none, juggle with these analogies, constantly seek new reconciliations, reach with happiness the incomprehensible, enjoys it and indulge in a weird intellectual dance around mysterious signs that are given all kinds of meanings, with even more ease than the origin of these signs is deferred to a few thousand years in the past.

One do not see men astray with equal ardor as when it comes to genealogy and especially genealogies of royal families. The spirit enters the noble relatives with the same insane love and lose itself merrily in the detail of illustrious lines as it loses itself in the distant symbols. Genealogies and symbols touch one another by the shields and cause in the most sober minds, curious transport which cease as soon as they return to other studies.

Tarot was the cause of ramblings as numerous as their multiple figures. But perhaps that they contain quite diverse elements, facets rather ingeniously arranged so that all contradictory imaginations that they engendered are true, from another perspective, because the perfect truth of nature reflects all the mistakes and makes them truths.

What is also striking in the study of Tarot is that this revealing book might have circulated through the centuries in the deep layers of humanity without being known and appreciated by those who studied the problems of science and metaphysics. Thus, there is a secret that is in the hands of charlatans and fortune-tellers, and is ignored by those who profess to be the great lights of men! Neither Plato nor Aristotle commented it in Greece. Neither Virgil nor Cicero reported it. And yet, the book with miraculous pictures circulated in Athens and Rome. One might think by reading the writings of wise men of Antiquity that Tarot was unknown in their time. There are no Tarot neither for Saint Augustine nor for Saint Thomas Aquinas. One might believe in the same way by reading the books of official wise men of our time, that there was no Tarot in the nineteenth century in Europe.

Neither Spinoza nor Renan nor Michelet nor Bergson have glanced at this book or if they did they have turned away from it disdainfully. The book with symbolic images takes an underground river to stroll. It is subject of witchcraft. It is handled only by impure hands of soothsayers or magicians accused of madness and many, only for having touched the painted cardboard hieroglyphs, were dressed with the hood and went up at the stake. There is a singular mystery.

Furthermore, those who have taken care of it, those who have believed in it, form a kind of spiritual family, are marked with a special predestination of misfortune. They were called visionaries and often mad. Their ideas of nature and life have been, more or less, the same. They have similar features as if by bowing to a common enigma they shaped themselves to the resemblance of the mystery and they caused themselves special fatalities.

The first was Gerolamo Cardano in the sixteenth century. He was visited by a familiar genius who was the same one who had assisted his father during his life, a family genius. Having bought one evening a book of Apuleius, even though he did not know Latin, it appeared the next day that he could read it fluently, his only desire to read Apuleius has given him the knowledge of the Latin language in one night. Despite such wonderful gifts, his life was one long struggle against poverty. He had a son, who was sentenced to death, a sentence which was announced to him by a small red spot on one of his nails and he felt obliged to cut an ear to his second son, as punishment for his debaucheries.

He had himself given him the example of a dissolute life, but he confessed all his sins with an incredible sincerity in a book: *De vita propria* because he attributed to confession, when it is complete, a power of purification. Scaliger, who considered him as one of the greatest minds of his time, accused him of having starved himself to death in order not to make the prediction he has made the day of his death lie, thanks to his astrological science. This accusation is free, because Gerolamo Cardano, who was a great astrologer, had in all probability known by the stars the moment for him to die the most favorable to his future development, and he took advantage of it with foresight.

It was Guillaume Postel[1] who found the relation of the word Tarot with Rota and who had the idea to dispose the cards of the major arcanas in the shape of a wheel, the key of the interpretations of these cards being in the initial form of the layout. He experienced extreme poverty. He fell in love with the Hebraic language to the extent of making himself rabbi for a time, which did not prevented him, after escaping from a prison of the Inquisition, to become chaplain in a hospital in Venice. There, he met an ecstatic, mother Jeanne, as he claims it, communicated him his spiritual substance and allowed him to enter in the higher worlds. He tried for a moment, at the college of France where he had a chair, to prove that the King of France, Charles IX was a descendant of the eldest son of Noah. Retired in the Saint-Martin des Champs convent, the universality of his knowledge made him so famous that he was forced to speak to his pupils from the top of a first floor window, and when he leaned, his longue silver beard almost touched the ground.

It should be noted that the whiteness of his beard was discussed three centuries later by Éliphas Lévi. This Cabbalist savant claimed, in his book *Histoire de la magie* that Guillaume Postel, after the death of mother Jeanne, had seen his wrinkles disappear and his hair and beard became black again. A fluidic life would have been given to him by the afterlife, by this discipline with which he remained in communion.

Court de Gébelin in the eighteenth century rediscovered Tarot and tried to explain it in one of the parts of his immense work *Le Monde Primitif* which remained unfinished and of which only nine volumes have been published. At the time of his death seven other volumes were

---

1 Guillaume Postel is the author among other things of the book *Absconditcmm a constitutione mundi clavis.*

written and ready to be published. They contained perhaps the final enlightenments on the meaning of Tarot.

But Court de Gébelin, like all Tarot enthusiasts, was hit by poverty and was forced to fight against it. Greedy creditors came to sell at auction his manuscripts and the end of the primitive world was scattered and lost in the hands of ignorant buyers. It is even said that it was a grocer who acquired most of the lots, probably to wrap cones salt or oil bottles. Such was the fate of the second part of the primitive world!

It seems that Tarots' science carries with it an unproductive power, a sterilizing element in the field of material life. No doubt it is written that the Cabbalistic wheel can only rotates with its dazzling images in a miserable attic ravaged by the winds of winter. There is perhaps a curse upon those who want to lift the veil of destiny. Perhaps Saul's word was not pronounced in vain. The Bohemians, to whom fall the task to spread Tarot on earth, remained a people of beggars.

The records of the Inquisition are full of names of magus and Cabbalists who have been imprisoned, tortured, burned because they have turned their eyes towards future, with the same ardor that others turn them towards the past. Etteilla, after that Court de Gébelin claimed to find the true meaning of Tarot, trade his humble fragment of science. If he made an exception to the rule and if he was not absolutely miserable (he charged 30 pounds for an horoscope and asked for 24 pounds to draw cards) his life was poisoned by the presence of a shrewish wife, he compared to Xantippe, which is a form of punishment of fate as formidable as the misery, the face of the bad wife being a living materialization of moral poverty.

The Cabbalist Éliphas Lévi, despite the vast size of his work, and even though he claimed to have found the unique key of Tarot (key he gives but which leaves the doors of mystery as inexorably closed) experienced distress during the end of his life. He was forced to emigrate to Elberfeld to find the daily bread at the house of one of his disciples. He was suffering from a kind of elephantiasis which made him die motionless in his chair, surrounded by the perpetual motion of all sacred and profane magic he had scrutinized the mysteries and whose formulas danced silently among the manuscripts that formed the circle of his dwelling.

Those who have business to promise to others more wealth by playing the major or minor arcanas were never favored by fortune. Is it their love of divination which led them to neglect the material things or is it because the circumstances deprived them of resources they thought to use from the divination to improve their lot? The two hypotheses may be also true because there is maybe a mysterious harmony between the poverty of daily life and a certain power of divination, regardless if that power comes from knowledge of Tarot or from a personal donation.

What is the why of this link? What is this rule of destinies which devotes to a bitter fight those who try to lift the veil that nature extended on the law of causes and effects. The rule exists and exceptions, such as the one of Swedenborg, who was a rich and esteemed savant, only confirms it.

The most natural explanation is that those who are seized by a passion, and the passion to decipher the future and know beyond normal bounds is the most powerful of all; neglect ordinary things of life, necessary approaches, the rites by which we keep the conquered place, and quickly see because of that negligence, destroy by themselves the advantages, situations, happiness.

But there is something else. This mysterious organization which, when it made grew animal species has, at the same time, developed plants to feed them, which establishes in nature proportions that scientific laws of evolution cannot explain, this immense occult provident may have set a time for the distribution of certain human knowledge. Nothing is more striking than the fact that when locusts and rats swarm, this expansion is suddenly stopped by an epidemic born of the excesses of the swarm. The law of nature does not want certain things. If it acts on grasshoppers and rats it must act on the human mind and act with even more attention than it is of a higher hierarchy. This action is carried out with a total lack of goodness in the human sense of the word. The outbreak of locusts, for the man who wants to unravel some mysteries whose cosmic plan has only provided the revelation for later, to its transposition into material poverty, in illness, sometimes madness.

Not only is there no reward for the selfless scientist, no human reward because it is always exposed to the ridicule and to contempt, but there is a danger, an elusive threat to which we refuse to believe because it is contrary to normal reason, a danger that comes from these mysterious powers always present around us, and all the more formidable that they are dear to us because we are part of them.

The Ark of Solomon's temple

Two peoples have used divination as an essential mean of their existence. Two peoples have been condemned to wander through the world, stripped of Ton's territory where Ton sows and where he collects means of life. These are Jews and Bohemians. Does the cause of this essential poverty come from the fact that those peoples have violated a human law, ripped a divine veil? Is there in the immense muddle of causes and effects a return game which strikes with poverty and evil the community which uses divination to increase its material power?

How to explain the relation of one to another? Science of causes and effects, whether it is in the history of nations or that of men, is completely unknown and what is called repercussions are never followed far away by those who apply them. Barely if everyone, by its personal law, discerns, and with how much difficulties, the mysterious path traced in his life, from cause to effect. One can only arise a problem without solving it.

The Ark of the Covenant of the Jews was sacred because apart from the Tables of the Law and the magic wand of Aaron it contained the way to see the future. This Ark, two and a half cubits in length was made of acacia wood, covered in gold leaf. On the solid gold cover were two carved cherubim, or sphinx with bodies of bulls and with wings of eagles, whose faces were turned toward each other. It was in the location situated between these two faces that the Israelites were waiting for the materialization of the divine spirit when they consulted the future. The spirit descended like a light on the Teraphim. Teraphim were figures carved in ivory or in precious stones. They represented characters, emblems, symbols of stars or elements. They were placed on a magical square called Ephod, between two signs in onyx, the Urim and the Thummim which had the meaning of yes and no and high priests drew deductions from the layout of the Teraphim. But the secret resided in the manner to operate these objects and it was only known by high priests.

When Jerusalem was taken by Nebuchadnezzar, Jeremiah took the Ark and hid it in the Mount Pisgah. According to a tradition, he could not find then the cave where he had left it. Yet, the Ark returned to the tabernacle of the Temple and, emanated from it, according to the tradition, a sort of halo of sanctity. It contained a magical force that killed a certain Uzzah, when he put out his hand on it. And if the legend says that David danced in front of the Ark it is because a spiritual power was contained in the strips of its gold, power which is communicated to initiates by the ritual game of the dance. Christianity has kept in some cases, the ritual of the dance. Savonarola made dance in the woods mystical dances to the monks of his community, accompanied with songs which his contemporaries found the words incomprehensible.

When the Romans of Titus destroyed the temple, the Ark was saved by priests, and greedy Romans only found a crude imitation of it behind the veil of purple and hyacinth.

What became the sacred Ark then? There is only a muddled legend about it. The Ark was saved by the Hillel family who brought it to Alexandria. When the Jewish quarter of this city was sacked by order of the bishop Cyril, the Hillel and some faithful took the Ark and sank with it in the deserts which are south of Thebes. A plundering tribe massacred the Hillel family and seized their possessions. The Jewish race had lost the inheritance of Moses. Three centuries later, Muhammad sent to Cairo Abu Bakr the truthful, to buy to a bazaar merchant precious objects he held from conductors of a southern caravan. How Muhammad had known the presence of the Ark in a Cairo bazaar. It should not be forgotten that Mohammed was in charge of magic. In possession of the talisman, the Arabs did not ask him divination but the power to defeat their enemies. The conquerors Okba and Abderame, traversed the entire North Africa, took hold of Spain and crossed the Pyrenees because they possessed the ineffable strength hidden in the blind gold by a millenary enchantment and by means of their faith they communicated with this force.

How the talisman slipped from their hands and who took it, the legend

ends there. One can assume that the Ark was hidden in all the castles
and fortresses where Arabs settled.

But the Ark contained a method of divination which was transmitted orally among the Jewish families wandering the world. The way to
dispose the Teraphim on the Ephod, the Teraphim were nothing more
than Jewish Tarot, arrived in Provence and was revealed in the sixteenth
century to the astrologer and physician Nostradamus.

Nostradamus was from a Jewish family and it was by using his astrological knowledge and by establishing the connection of stars with
Cabbalistic Tarot that he was able to make his famous prophesies. His
story has often been treated and I will not report it here.

What should be remembered of him is the great wisdom he had attained. Normally, he should have been burned. He was, on the contrary,
honored by kings and even by the Church. He was the guest of many
abbeys of which he consulted the libraries. Catherine de' Medici sum-
moned him to court and Charles IX, went to pay him a visit in Salon.
He had had the prudence to convert to Christianity, almost at the same
time when Guillaume Postel was mad enough to become rabbi.

The most important thing to remember is that he destroyed the documents of divination he possessed. He probably measured the danger
they represented for all man who had not attained the degree of superior knowledge.

Nostradamus had a son, astrologer like him. He wrote him the de-
termination he had taken not to transmit him this priceless heritage.
The history relates and reproduces the letter without saying how it was
received.

This son had a taste so great for predictions that, being in Le Pouzin,
fortified town in the Vivarais, when the royal troops made siege of it,
he announced haphazardly that the assailants will set fire to the city
when they will seize it. The assailants entered in Le Pouzin without
setting it on fire. The astrologer tried by himself to set the fire. He was
caught at the moment when he wanted to force the destiny to fulfill to
his imprudent views and he was put to death.

Along with Nostradamus disappeared the last traces of astrological

Teraphim, Moses had handled on the gold of the Ark, between the Cherubim with bodies of bulls.

The mission of the Bohemians

Between all the names they have received, the Bohemians have been called Mohani, from the noun of the goddess of poverty in India. This is the one that suits them best.

The Bohemians have not left the deep layers of earth. There is a Bohemian's mission which has not been treated. Mr. Saint-Yves d'Alveydre[1], author of so many "missions". The mission of the Bohemian was to transport through the world, across the wretched classes, the book of Tarot, so that an awaken soul, but chained to poverty, unable to participate to the riches of science and locked philosophies in the libraries, yet found an abstract of knowledge, easy to reach and that intuition was sufficient to illuminate.

The Bohemians have faithfully fulfilled their mission. Maybe because the characteristic of this people, declared by all as deposed without evidence or reason, is to be faithful. They are faithful to their religion, they worship under an apparent Christianity, to their friendships, to their oaths, even to their costume, which they obtain despite times and places the multicolored rags.

Here is an example of this unusual attachment to the given word.

In 1667, France had made responsible a certain Pierre Durois to study secretly the military forces of the German Empire. To do so he mingled with a group of Bohemians, imitated their manners and language. But when he was about to enter in France there was a fire in the small town of Patok in Hungary, near which encamped the group to which he belonged. Bohemians were accused of setting voluntarily the fire, accusation which was standard in Europe, when there was a given disaster. Pierre Durois was suspected of being a spy. For nine years, his companions were kept in prison and tortured, and none of them con-

---

1 This false great man lost himself in social ramblings he turned around the word: synarchy.

sented to betray him. After nine years, they were all hanged but they remained faithful until the end.

The Bohemians had no lawyer to plead their case, no poet to magnify the freedom of their lives. The history of the race without a country, without eloquence to express its misery, without sufficient intelligence which allows to find in oneself the consolation to evil, without outrage to revolt and die, is one of the most painful tragedies of the human history. For them the injustice never stopped, it trained without this mercy which is given to ordinary beggars, and this injustice still continues.

"Their women are beautiful, well made and brought to the lubricity" said naively J. A. Vailland, author of a rare book where their defense is taken. And he also says by speaking of them "sutlers, spies, looters, leaving in common and dealing with the virginity of their daughters". "Ignorant and vicious men" says Papus, who has wrote a book on the Tarot of the Bohemians, and Grellmann, their main historian: "How would it be possible that noble and virtuous feelings could exist in souls full of baseness and vice". Every time they are mentioned somewhere it is with wilting words, by writers who do not base on any study of this race, nothing, except the reputation of few chickens disappeared after the passage of their carriages on the roads.

The Bohemians came from India. Their origin has been discussed for a long time, but the relationship of their language and of their customs with Tzingaris from the Malabar Coast and southern India, shows, with no possibility of doubt, that there was their first homeland. Furthermore they still exist in the land of the Marathas, similar in every way to their brothers of Granada, in Spain, less the simulacrums of religion.

It is when Timur, the destroyer of cities and peoples, the one of whom the legend says that he was born with hands full of blood, strut his fury in northern of India, that they slipped in Europe. One does not see them pass.

But they suddenly start to proliferate almost everywhere. Their martyr started as soon as they asked hospitality to Western Christians.

It would be an enumeration impossible to make to want to recall the injustices they were stricken by. There were not penned in ghettos. There were not even granted to make fire at the edge of the road and that miserable fire of their food served sometimes as a pretext for a charge of idolatry. If they lit the fire in the evening, it was to worship it!

What one reproached them more than the flights, were the witchcraft practices. The charge that overwhelmed them was invisible, like the devilish power. All edicts of expulsion or death issued by the judges of the various countries are therefore conclusive, unassailable reason for the stupidity of time. It was this reason that justified the pious hatred attached to them. On their way, it is said that children are dying and flocks languish. They leave a smell of sulfur, a hellish wake. They are the representatives of the Devil, a devil in a caravan, family, with an evening pot, many children, colored scarves, a devil even more terrible, that he imagined a caricature of a family in rags.

In Spain they were assimilated to Moors and sentenced to banishment and death by Isabelle the exterminator, all historians of all countries have continued to glorify and they have called her great.

In Germany, Maximilian I, decreed that it was not a crime for a good German to kill a Bohemian. As they discover gold powder in rivers and can pay a tribute with this gold, Maria Theresa, Queen of Bohemia and Hungary, the firm and magnanimous Maria Theresa, tolerates them in the Carpathians, by effect of his great mercy. But, under very severe penalties, she forbids them to speak their language without nevertheless teaching them another; as they only know their own, they are forced to express themselves by signs as mute persons!

In Utrecht, in 1545, a Bohemian who did not leave early enough the city after the order of expulsion was shaved, whipped until he bled and had both nostrils split, strange and rare punishment, related to the sense of smell, probably invented for the occasion, in order to spare him cooking odors, so cruel for a wandering and hungry man.

In a small principality of the German empire whose prince was a great hunter, a Bohemian woman and her child were thrown in a wood and she was hunted as a game.

In Castile, one night, a shepherd of a certain overweight bumped into Bohemians who were sitting and eating at a crossroad. They invited him fraternally to share this meal. He agreed, he ate, he drunk and then took his leave of his hosts and returned home. But he remembered that one of them has said, during the meal, under the pretence of cheerfulness: "In truth, here is a very fat fellow". He ran to see the judge. There was no doubt! They have measured his corpulence to eat him! The Bohemians were imprisoned and were condemned for an intention of cannibalism.

This accusation was frequent. In order to prove it, in 1620[1] Don Martin de Fajardo, judge in Jaraicejo, took few Bohemians aimlessly in a group, put them to torture and made them confess what he wanted, also a feast made with a Franciscan monk who had disappeared and whose disappearance had to be justified.

All it took was for their stick to have some circular folds of the wood in order to see the form of a thyrsus and a testimony of paganism. And the most familiar crime of those *strigoi* or vampires was to steal the shadows of the passersby, or rather the copies of the shadows, each having at any time the proof that he still had his shadow, to roll and take them into their carriages and to use them for spells and enchantments.

While reading the history of this long martyrdom where only tortures, gibbets and stakes are destined for Bohemians, one can wonder how it is possible that at that time there was no great movement of pity, an invincible momentum of indignation from a just and enlightened mind, able to act on his contemporaries, whether being cardinal, prince or philosopher. But never! No one was moved! No one dared to shout that there was no such race so deposed, even being thief by nature, loving vermin that covered it, delighting to open graves to strip the dead and eat carrions, that could not be saved by a mercy gesture, a drop of love. Nobody made the gesture, no one had shed the luminous tear that would have been the star the of wanderings.

When one reads the history of the Bohemians in the book of the German Grellmann, one remains confused as the historian who has looked at this long succession of miseries and has recounted it, reporting the dates of the injustices and the locations where they took place, not only did not have the smallest movement of protest, but again ex-

1 Vaillant. *Histoire Vrai des vrais Bohémiens.*

claimed himself on the utility of the coercive measures, found them excellent, resulting from the perfect honesty of societies, wanted more severe punishments.

And yet one is still surprised that such misery might have been supported by human hearts, without breaking. One cannot help to think once more about what that Bohemian who, scourged from city to city, because he was Bohemian, body ravaged and forming only one wound, went back through all those cities of ordeal to return to the first where he had been promised that he would be burned if he would come back and where he returned indeed in order to claim the made promise.

Yet, during a random speech, the miserable and insensitive Grellmann dropped an explanation of this enigma of suffering borne in contempt. And this explanation with indifference, is the following:

"Despair is unknown to them."

Is it possible? One should meditate on this affirmation of the conscientious and narrow-minded man who, with his soul of stone, has studied the wandering race, its reactions and its possibilities.

Thus, there would be a people to whom despair would be unknown! A man could return from town to town in order to be scourged again, knowing a Calvary which has no divine hope, to find at the end a stake and quietly climb it, amid spits, with the serene feeling of its own vileness. And there would be no despair in him!

The people ignoring the despair would be the one who have never made the effort to attach to a particular land, with its same climate, same smell, its similar vegetation, a house of stone or wood, with the regularity of its shape and the prison of its walls. The people who did not accept the pact with the divine law itself, would be the people possessing Tarot, the book of life and death, the people whose children have the faculty to know daily their personal relationship with the movement of stars in the sky.

No despair for the one that is not bound! His body can be ripped and he will make a long journey with the prospect of being burned alive. In truth, it opens up a vast horizon of thought.

When I had closed the books where is recorded the history of those that no one has praised, unbelievers who turn the baptism into derision and do not take care of their bodies or their souls, I could not help saying:

- Glory to those anti-citizens, these men who could not enslave themselves to any law, those born rebels, these unlucky magicians, these vendors of cheap witchcraft. They did not believe the fertility of the land and have not sown wheat, but their face was turned towards the stars every night and they have received from it advices and secret words. They may have had all the vices of which we have accused them, but wickedness and lack of forgiveness of men exceeded ten thousand times their capacity of evil, it was so great, so inconceivable, so inhuman that it placed around their visionaries hair covered with lice, a halo of evil that illuminates them forever.

Astral and divinatory entities

The ancient tradition dictates that the world has been created from an egg. One can compare the book of seventy-eight pages to a spiritual egg. Just as a seed contains all the future possibilities that will develop by combined terrestrial and solar power, so the Tarot carry in its images every possible combination of human and divine thought. And as the material creation, the world of causes is in the mind, the one who will wield the spiritual beam of causes will also experience the world of effects.

Tarot was also employed for divination because of all time, men have been eager to lift the veil of their upcoming future[1].

But how can human destiny manifest itself through 78 cards? The one who consults Tarot may have in some cases and depending on the person who wields Tarot, a forecast on the events of his life, erroneous predictions sometimes, but in other moments strikingly accurate. The fact that some images come out when a man questions them, and that these images are in connection with what has to happen to him, is here a singular mystery, but which is in any case indisputable. A clairvoyance is exercised through time by the intervention of Tarot.

"There is not only, in the divinatory fact, a subjective gift of the operator. There is indisputably an objective value of the operation. Give the arcanas to anyone, if he is capable to focus his mind to ask only one question at a time, and tell him to spread them on a table in a given order, or better, do it instead of him. If you know how to read the chart which appears, the answer to the question asked will emerge with an irresistible force, sometimes a clarity of comments of which you will

1 Tarot has been extensively studied nowadays in interesting works by Falconnier, Papus, Bourgeat, Oswald Wirth, George Muchery, Alta and Maxwell. Falconnier has found an Egyptian tarot, Papus the one of Bohemians, C. Muchery, an astrological Tarot, Oswald Wirth the Tarot of the Imagiers du moyen âge, inspired by Stanislas de Guaita.

remain dazzled."

Thus says Mr. Gabriel Trarieux.

On the other hand, doctor Osty who struts on all the occult phenomena an inexorable observation lamp, while recognizing that the divinations are indisputable, when the clairvoyant have a gift, says "that if the cards have a role in the divination, this role is certainly not to provide directly knowledge." According to him, cards or Tarot are only external signs, the media on which the faculty of the seer rests.

Of these two opinions which seems contradictory, which one is true? Their contradiction is perhaps only visible, and viewed from a certain angle they meet.

One must first remember a suggestive sentence of Zohar.

"A tradition teaches us that we must tell these illusions only to people who loves us. They will be realized because the friends to whom we will tell them will interpret them favorably[1]."

Thus one should only ask to scrutinize the future by the means of Tarot to a seer of whom one is loved or at least, for the love of a soothsayer is rare, only to a soothsayer with whom we established some friendly relationships.

Sympathy is the unseen atmosphere in which will best manifest the phenomenon of strange appearance - because it is not well known, and of evocative order, which occurs when one wants to speak the silent language of Tarot.

Reading Tarot is a kind of evocation. In reality, the one who would want to read them conscientiously should have prepared for it by hours of meditation, a food made of pure foods and a total chastity because it is only under those conditions that the human being divests himself of these rude emanations and is able to communicate with forces or beings from another plane.

Communicate! Here is the great problem. There is no doubt that the universe is inhabited by various lives and invisible creatures, whether these creatures have forms or not. What makes us the conception of these incredible creatures is that we always represent them with heads

1 *Zohar*, t.II (1.200).

and torsos, similar to ours. But one can imagine living beings devoid of sensible forms, spread as waves, vibrating as currents and having a separate existence, with a different mode of consciousness from ours.

But these entities are nonexistent for us as we do not have the ability to communicate with them. The Tarot may be a mode of communication.

Anyhow, these entities are not omniscient and they will only let us know what they know by themselves, if however they want to, in case they would have good will.

The reading of Tarot is perhaps, that is to say the way to communicate, a matter of higher faculty, this faculty that Mr. Paul Le Cour, in a remarkable book[1], has called the Aisthesis.

Thanks to this faculty, similar to the inspiration of the artist, in the metaphysical state of the philosopher, the man can get in touch with a different way of life, a spiritual mode where one is among the causes and where, consequently, one can see the effects, at least, to some extent.

"The knowledge which comes down from above in the soul is more excellent than all those that can be obtained by the mere exercise of the mind" said the wise Proclus.

A knowledge which comes down from above! There is obviously no above. But above means: more subtle world.

If one has access to this world, one can participate to these forces, wield them, use them. In this world one can find entities, which are creatures, in the ordinary sense of the word, but creatures which have suffered the law of their spiritual environment. This law is expansion. Unlike man, condensed creature of flesh and blood around an axis of bones, these beings are widespread, have no shape, or an inaccessible one to our understanding. There is a connection between these kinds of psychic forces and Tarot. Tarot is their language.

If one consider the root of the word Tarot, Tar means polar star in Sanskrit, one will understand that Tarot has a connection with stars whose influence determines human destinies. The entities of the spiritual world which express themselves by Tarot are only those whose force determines these destinies. To the extent that, man's destiny depends

1 Paul Le Cour: *Le septième sens: l'aisthesis.*

on stars, the entities can speak because they know. To the extent that, by the use of his freedom, man escapes to the influences of heaven, the entities are ignorant and they are wrong. However, one never notice, or so I believe, conscious or deliberate error. They do not make jokes. The entities that one can both call astral and divinatory, are likely deprived of consciousness or, if they have one, they do not exercise it on a human level.

Tarot has therefore a magical character. They allow someone who has prepared himself for it to be in relation with psychic forces of a different plan than ours. But most of the times, consulted Tarot make no reasonable divinatory answer. It is that the ignorant soothsayer has not tried to refine his soul and has the pretention of wanting to penetrate, with his impurity and the deformities of his desires, in the subtle country of the incomplete astral knowledge. This lack of preparation is the main cause of the frequent silence of Tarot.

But even when the language responds, when the consulted soothsayer, having temporarily abolished his sensibility and his reasoning faculties, interacts with entities of stellar order, these ones can only say what is within their power. They know, for example that an event is inevitable determined and they announce it.

But by announcing it, they create a new cause, in the entanglement of causes and effects, and this cause can change the inevitable character of the event, and allow the one it concerns to shirk to it. Thus, the astral entities, despite their shocking and total indifference, sometimes intervene in terrestrial events and disturb the order that they had themselves planed.

The parent entities

When Ton wants to consult Tarot, Ton ordinarily goes to see a lady of a certain age, who lives at the back of the courtyard, on the third floor, on the right. This lady rose from reading Papus and Léon Denis and is imbued with spiritualistic ideas. She strives to comply immediately his speech to your desires, she has mixed with some elementary morality, based on family duties, morality that of spiritualism.

Alas! It is not this lady that one should consult, but hardworking and chaste wise, full of science and intuition. It is a pity that Tarot is tarnished by a certain defamation and that it is not Einstein, the astronaut Jeans or the mathematician Eddington who look at their enigma.

The initiators of man, those whose intelligence has shown in the dawn of time, after having thrown the seeds of thought, have undoubtedly deposited in Tarot a form of language allowing to communicate with infinitely superior entities to divine entities, of which we have spoken. These entities, which can also be called Gods, which ones are they?

Everything is hierarchy in the world and there is a superposition of forces and powers which are stretched ad infinitum. The creative ideas, the essential laws, are perhaps beings spread in solar systems, being so immense that the entities of our planets seem to them to be child entities endowed with tiny beams. Why man would not have a mean to have the reflection of these parent entities, the shortcut of these generative laws?

If an ant, by transporting methodically grains on a flat surface, was drawing a straight line, then an angle, then a triangle and a circumference, it would come despite its small size to correspond with a human God who, if he is neither very powerful nor very smart, in relation to his own immensities, has even enough power to make in its sole the happiness or misfortune of the ant world. Anyhow, this mathematician ant would create an instructive correspondence with a universe different from its own, it would learn the existence of cosmic giants and it would allow the ant to discover new insights on its insect destiny.

Just like for us. Geometric figures of the ant are Tarot. Through them, one could see, not miserable forecasts on our journeys, our unions with spouses, or the car accidents to which we are exposed, but the knowledge of essential laws of the world and especially the direction that we have to give to our inner being, to our true self, which is the only important thing.

The capital secret is locked up in Tarot, the secret which allows to come out from the circle of the earth where the soul is voluntarily locked. But can only read it the one who is not blinded by the idea of present or the immediate future which is only a present in preparation.

Behind the images with which the intuitive announce, to those who consults them, the events of their earthly life, is found a transcendent geometry of ideas by which inspired philosophers will teach us one day, spiritual operations through which it will be possible to us to attain the upper regions of the mind.

The door of death leads only to some conditions very difficult to accomplish. When this door is crossed, once all the known conditions have been fulfilled, who knows if one does not realize with horror that one has forgot an essential point, a method of direction proper to heavens, without which one remains in uncertainty and darkness! It is then that maybe one should rush forward once again in the cycle of forms, obey to the obscene attraction of birth, to come learn the secret imprudently neglected!

There is a language which allows to access directly to the pure realm of thoughts, where everything is order and beauty, intelligence, peace and communion with the divine models. The one who knows this sacred alphabet enters directly into this realm of harmony because one does not penetrate it by any door, but by a reaction of the mind.

What was hidden there, reveals itself. One contemplates there the spiritual dual of the Parthenon, under the visible brutality of Hindu temples, behind the trunks of elephants of Ganesha Gods, between the floating ears of Krishna Gods, one sees the metaphysical subtleties in the eternal sense. There harmonizes contradictions. The Greek portico is at the same time a Christian cloister and Plato has a conversation there with Shankaracharya. The numbers of Pythagoras are exactly those of the nails that Jakob Böhme plunged into soles, when he was a shoemaker. The glasses of eyeglasses polished by Spinoza are of the same quality as those through which Ptolemy looked at the sky. The forms of Michelangelo vibrate like music and Beethoven sonatas become statues. Landscapes can be heard as well as seen and the ambient love is drawn by the play of breathing. This is the realm of parent entities, the Pleroma of intelligences, the circumference where stroll endlessly the chosen ones. And these chosen ones are not those who have received God's grace, but those who have voluntarily given themselves this grace.

* * *

An entire volume would be required to explain one by one the images of Tarot. I will content myself by indicating that the essential idea of the liberation of the human soul is the 21st card, the one who is designated as the most important because it ends the third set of cards of the major arcanas.

It has been explained by Mr. Maxwell who has contradicted on this point other learned writers, as Éliphas Lévi.

This 21st card represents a naked young woman, with a human soul, who only touches the earth with the tip of her left foot and rises towards the sky.

She is surrounded, from all four corners of the figure, by the four symbolic creatures, the lion, the bull, the eagle and the man. But here the man is replaced by an angel. It is the symbol of the change wrought by the soul, leaving the human kingdom to enter the mysterious next reign, that an image of a winged and chubby child symbolizes imperfeclty and which is the reign of the man delivered from the matter.

THE SECRET OF BUDDHA AND JESUS

The Secret of Buddha and Jesus

It belongs to the ordinary man to go further than the promises of his gods. Divine promises are insufficient either because they were vague or poorly worded, or they reached us only through the transformations of narrow-minded disciples.

It is a narrow conception of morals that still veil the teachings of the great prophets. The disciples only dream of bishop's titles, papal honors. To be worthy of these honors they conform themselves to the morals of vulgar, and they diminish beautifully destructive instructions of visionaries who saw and who spoke with the great freedom that only gives the loneliness of the genius in the highlands of mind.

The Nirvana Buddha is illuminated by a gray light where one is not sure will shine the light of consciousness, this lamp where was poured oil so carefully and with pain, of which we have seen the clarity faint to all the winds. Isn't Nirvana a similar serenity to that of sleep? My God! Keep us from a too peaceful state where there would be no more space for pity!

The kingdom of God of Jesus does not offer more certainty. Come to my father, has he been constantly saying. When a friend, makes you such an invitation in daily life, one cannot help but to represent itself a strict father, likely on relationships that can have his son and a house where one will be penetrated by an atmosphere of austerity. The son who loved to drink wine and see spread precious perfume on his feet, will cease to be a fraternal companion in the presence of the too serious Father. Ah! A free and small private house where guests could keep all the ease of friendship!

Is there a secret more high than the one that have passed the divine beings? Have the Druids known it, has it traveled the world as the emerald symbol of the Grail, is it in the figures of the Tarot? And is that secret the salvation of man?

Work out his salvation! What a powerful and evocative word. I have never been able to say it without a shudder. But where is the way of this salvation? As they are happy and marked with the sign of the choose ones, those who never think about it! Or rather not, what a miserable flock of blind slaves only occupied with their food and their sex!

Salvation is somewhere, it has to be found, by running here and there, where there are creatures or things likely to generate intuitions, to extract it with effort from the profound roots of his soul. And one cannot be deceived by the one who hypocritically says that by being a good husband, a good father, a good citizen, a good son, or whatever. Good in every conceivable forms, one makes normally his salvation and will sit alongside gods, gods surrounded probably by children, fathers, wives, all as perfectly good.

Ordinary morality is a trap. It is the single penny the miser gives each year to the poor, to dispense himself with charitable action. Who knows if this daily altruism, as recommended by all the rules of religions and philosophies is not the great temptation imposed by these two sisters' goddesses, these two beloved goddesses who do not have eyes and almost any face, the ignorance and stupidity?

Salvation is beyond the Buddhist conception of Nirvana and the God's Kingdom of Jesus. It is beyond these vast horizons and so close to us that one can touch it with its hand. It does not only consist in the detachment from earthly life as stated by Buddha and Jesus. Because, like it or not, the conclusion of their wisdom is that one should go sit in the woods under a tree, like an ascetic, or rotate between the pillars of a cloister, like a monk, rejecting life with dances, his acts of generation and his joyous exhilarations.

Salvation is in the love of life, but of a higher life and more beautiful life than the one which is within our grasp of the circular extent of this planet of water and granite. It requires both to love life and reject it, participate in the essence and to strip off the bark. One must get out of this too heavy world and conqueror a lighter one.

But how one can do so? What is the common thread? There is in the emotion given by beauty, something of which the depth has never been measured. Perfection of a statue, a music or this undefined lightning that indicates the compositions of words of a poem! It is in the sense of beauty that consciousness and beatitude come together, that is to say the higher states to which one can claim, states that seem to contradict and blend to a certain height. Neither Buddha nor Jesus spoke of the beauty and the poet Plato wanted to banish poets from his republic. So? Since it is difficult to agree with his teachers and what audacity it takes to accuse them of error or oversight!

No, it is not possible for man to be thrown into an insensitive matrix to discuss it, to dream of justice and disappear for no reason. It has aids somewhere, only he does not know the way to call them. When he has entered the circle of the living manifestation of various forms nourished by sun and darkness, he has received a talisman allowing him to get out of this circle. But he lost it. He sank into an endless maze and he walks and he cries. But the talisman is perhaps at his feet.

It is perhaps in the emerald chalice of the Grail where the blood has not dried, perhaps in the seventy-eight painted images, perhaps in the angle of a ray of sunlight reflected by still water. Perhaps one simply needs to kneel? Maybe one should rather stand and head held high?

Just as when I was a child and besides until an advanced age, I could not understand why the North Star is the only motionless in the sky, and I do not understand what exactly salvation is and a very simple reasoning could possibly make me understand it.

And I say in other minutes that it is not necessary to be saved. Salvation involves the idea that some are not saved and that if we do nothing, we are lost. And if those who did nothing were the happiest? If it was because of this that men who knew, or were supposed to know, were so deliberately ambiguous in their words.

And if oneself we were saved and if those we loved were not? If salvation was as cold as the solitude of the egoist?

The path of salvation is full of darkness, of harrowing regrets, reproaches, just as a liaison with a young woman, when one is twenty. And it contains a similar trap. As we have doubted of the beloved creature, we doubt the path we follow, we are scared that it leads to nowhere.

Superior men we encounter will strengthen us in this doubt, just as they once said that your beloved cheated on you with everyone.

The key is to never give any credence to the words of men who are supposed to be superior, never to admit the possibility of doubt.

Because everything is certainty. The legends are true, truer than history. These are the exact documents that disguise the truth and the Indians of the time of the Vedas were right, who were not involved in chronology and only relied in the verb, because it had wings.

Glancing back at my reading and my approaches in pursuit of salvation, examining the taste of the wonderful that made me admire sometimes charlatans and chasing chimeras, now that certainty is in me, I think that even if there were no secret, even if no one knew if the Hindu Rishis were ignorant old men of the Himalayan mountains, if the Druids in their beard of convention had only been occupied by picking mistletoe to make herbal teas, if the chalice of the Grail had been empty and also had been empty the ark the Teraphim, if all the prophets had lied, if the magicians had been only illusionists and the saints deluded persons, if Apollonius of Tyana had not existed, if there had been no knights of the Round Table, no Rosy Cross, no insider brothers, I think it would be appropriate even so to honor the Rishis, the Druids, the Knights of the Round Table, I think one should go meditate at Montségur in Ariège and find Shambhala in the Gobi desert; sculpt or paint hastily the Teraphim, the Swastika and Solomon's seals.

Because it is thanks to magus, initiated brothers, talismans, magical chalices, symbolic signs, winged angels, bearded enchanters, that ardor is born, of magical nature, which sends you one day in the region where the sky has no more stars because we are part of its light and where the soul is finally quiet, because it has found salvation.

Discovery Publisher is a multimedia publisher whose mission is to inspire and support personal transformation, spiritual growth and awakening. We strive with every title to preserve the essential wisdom of the author, spiritual teacher, thinker, healer, and visionary artist.